For Raymond

A Sister's Memoir

Pat Lingenfelter

Acknowledgements

$\mathscr{I}$ thank my husband and my son for surviving numerous months without me while I worked on this book. Never once did I hear a complaint from either one. I am especially grateful to my sister, T. Lynn, who has always been supportive to me. I greatly appreciate my sister, K. Mary, for her candor and faith that I "would do the right thing." My Aunt Sara boosted my morale when it was waning with her support and encouraging letters. Thank you to my many friends for their support. They are too numerous to mention in this short passage. A special thanks goes out to my mother who never faltered in her love, even when my emotions were running amuck. I'm eternally grateful to Cindy Matheis who was my mentor, my pep squad and my editor. I couldn't have done this book without her. Lastly, I would like to thank my brother, Raymond, who inspired me with his gentle ways and his never-ending love. This book is for Raymond.

Preface

My brother, Raymond's, life hasn't ended with his passing away. I feel his constant presence. I sense he's watching over me, compelling me and at times even facilitating me to tell his story. You see, my brother was severely retarded and unable to utter a single word. I must be his voice. I must tell his tale. If I don't, it will lie buried with him forever, and the world will go on as it did. I couldn't live with myself if I let that happen.

At first I wrote for vengeance, but time and reflection have given me a different perspective and I see there is much more to Raymond's story than a vehicle for retribution.

I've thought long and hard about what Raymond wants me to say and how to say it. I'm not an accomplished author. I'm not an eloquent speaker. I'm just a sister who loved her brother— I can only tell Raymond's story through my own crude words about my personal struggle with what happened to him. That makes this tale a one-sided version. Nonetheless, it is the truth as I saw it under the most trying of circumstances.

In looking back, I'm sure that most of those who took care of Ray did the best they could for him. No medical malpractice was uncovered. No laws were broken. Well-intended legislation and the most modern of medical procedures trapped my brother and my family in a scenario that no one should have to endure.

It is not my intention to point fingers or to implicate any person or institution; therefore, I have changed all of the names of the people and facilities involved, except for those of Raymond and myself. It doesn't matter in what city my family lived, in what facilities Raymond stayed, or the names of his caretakers. What matters is what he, the most innocent and helpless of human beings, was forced to endure.

I regret that in not using real names I will not be able to thank publicly those who treated my brother humanely. There also were many who helped to carry my family and me through our hellish ordeal. My family has thanked them privately and is eternally grateful to each and every one of them.

The writing of this book has been a long and difficult road for me. Sometimes I stumbled. At times I fell off of the road, but every time I faltered in my writing, someone happened along to prod me, to remind me of how important Raymond's story is. With each difficulty I prayed for guidance and waited with an open mind. My prayers were always answered, sometimes in unconventional ways, but answered just the same.

One of those unconventional ways was through a woman I stumbled upon in a store that sold angels. She told me that Raymond's story is his gift to me. I'd like to think of Raymond and his story as a gift to everyone, a gift I'd like to share with you.

A wise man once said that every society is judged by how it treats its least fortunate

My brother, Raymond, was born on May 28, 1951. He was my parents' second child. My mother tells me that he was a beautiful baby. The delivery was flawless. There wasn't a mark on him, and there was no indication that anything was wrong with him. It took my mother months to convince doctors that Ray wasn't developing like a normal child. After much arguing, Ray's doctors finally agreed that my mom was not just a neurotic. Ray was severely mentally retarded. Tests showed that he also had epilepsy and cerebral palsy.

Eight years after Raymond came into this world, my mother was pregnant with her sixth child. She hadn't had a full night's sleep since Raymond was born. My father worked two jobs to feed his ever-growing family. The years of endless care and interrupted sleep were taking a toll on my parents. They decided to place Ray in the nearest New York State developmental center for the handicapped, run by the New York State Developmental Disabilities Services Office (NYS DDSO). It was an hour-and-a-half ride by car from their house in upstate New York.

Raymond was seldom mentioned in our house, but during a rare moment, my mother opened her heart to me and talked about Ray's living conditions. She told me, "One time, I went for a tour of where the kids slept. There was one big room where the beds were all in rows, with the head of one bed touching the foot of another. The room they ate in was connected. They never left that floor unless someone from the family came and took them out. They stayed there all day long. The kids looked clean, but the smell of that place was so bad it permeated everything, even Ray's clothes.

"I remember when your sister, Lynn, was born [the sixth child]. I couldn't go to see Ray for two months. When I went to visit him at that developmental center, they brought him out on a gurney. They said he had been sick and had stopped walking. I was so upset that your dad took me to a rose festival in the town where the developmental center was. Ray never walked again after that.

"One time they wanted to cut the muscles in Ray's legs to straighten them so it would be easier for them to change him. That was after his legs became frozen in a sitting position. I told them no. He just had had surgery to take a growth off his back that was growing into his spine, and they wanted to do that to him. Then another time they wanted to put all the mentally retarded people in with the psychiatric patients. Can you imagine how they would have been treated? I went around with a petition to stop that.

"I was so glad when Ray was moved to a new place. It was so much nicer. There were two kids to a room. There wasn't that awful smell, and the nurses were so much more pleasant. A friend of mine told me she was visiting that place and went by Ray's room. She saw him crying and a nurse was comforting him. It just broke my heart when I heard that."

My mother's recollections made me remember the few times I went to visit Ray at that new facility. I felt like I was walking through the portal to hell or what my juvenile mind envisioned hell to be. After going down the long winding driveway that passed through acres of land, we entered a big two-story brick building with screened-in porches. To get to Ray's ward, we had to walk through long hallways. The hallways were lined with kids in wheelchairs parked outside their rooms. Kids with huge heads that they couldn't hold up, kids with deformed eyes that they couldn't see out of, kids with limbs crippled up from God knows what ailments. Some would rock back and forth, a constant mindless rocking that drove me crazy to watch.

If I blocked the sight of those poor wretched creatures from my eyes, I'd still hear the moans and unintelligible noises made by them as we passed through the halls. Those sights and sounds made a disturbing impression on my vulnerable little mind that made my heart scream and my stomach wretch. My young mind couldn't fathom back then that these people were being well taken care of and weren't suffering. All I saw was their grotesqueness.

Once we got through the "portal to hell," we came to Raymond's ward, where they kept the more mobile residents. They were gentle, curious people who kept walking past Ray's room to see who was visiting their buddy. Ray, who was nosy himself, loved all of the activity on his floor. He would just smile and let out a yelp of glee when anyone he knew came by.

My last memory of Ray in an institution was when I went with my mother to see him while he was in a psychiatric hospital. He had broken his leg, and the state policy then was that wards of the state with mental retardation were to be treated in psychiatric hospitals instead of regular hospitals. He had been in there for three months while he had surgery on his broken leg, then waited for it to heal, then had surgery to re-break it because it hadn't healed correctly, then waited for it to heal again.

To get into the hospital, you had to ring a buzzer, wait for someone to come unlock the door, and then it was re-locked after you went through it. I remember the panic I felt as I realized I was being locked in with the mentally ill patients.

Mom and I found Ray donning a hospital gown and sitting in his wheelchair all alone in a corner. Ray grinned as soon as he heard my mother's voice. His radiant smile revealed a tongue covered with a brown film and breath that smelled like a sulfur pit. I couldn't get within a few feet of him without my stomach doing flip-flops.

When our visit was over, I bolted out of that room, through the doors as they were unlocked, and into the great outdoors to gulp in the fresh air. That smell lingered in my nose for hours and in my memory forever. On the way home I cried silently for Ray and all the poor souls locked up in that hospital and at the mercy of those caretakers. A young mind is a very impressionable thing.

After that visit my life went on. I married, had a son, worked full time, and went back to school. There were a thousand excuses I could give for paying little thought to Raymond. But those repulsive encounters were the main reason why I didn't take the time to see him. The years had sped by—twenty, to be exact—before I again visited Ray. During that time, the last facility in which Ray lived was closed, and the residents were put into group homes. Ray's group home was about an hour's ride from my parents' house.

Ray had become gravely ill, and I was taking my mother to see him. He had been in and out of the hospital numerous times. Doctors couldn't figure out what was wrong with Ray. They just kept doing tests and sending him back to his group home as soon as he could keep food down and stop crying out in pain. He was diagnosed with esophageal reflux disease, but he suffered from much more than that.

I felt like such a horrible sister when I realized that it had been so long since I had seen my brother. I hadn't found the time to see Ray in all of those years. I could endure the unpleasantness once more to see him when he was so ill.

I was surprised when we arrived at the group home and I saw that it was set up just like a regular home but on a grander scale. The aide guided Mom and I through spacious halls with bedrooms off of them, furnished in bright colors. In the middle of the house was a big combined dining room and living room. The dining room had several long tables to accommodate all of the residents. The living room had comfy, overstuffed couches and chairs. The shelves on the walls were filled with crafts the residents had either made or bought. There was a big aquarium and a cat that snuggled with everyone.

Ray was the only resident there when we arrived to visit. The others had been sent off to daycare. He was in his wheelchair, facing away from us toward the TV, when we entered the living room.

I went over to see Ray as my mom talked to the plump caretaker. I knew that Ray's curly locks had grayed from seeing pictures of him that the group home periodically sent to my mother; but the pictures didn't show just how crippled up he had become over the years. He wasn't at all like the beautiful little boy in the picture I had on my shelf at home.

Ray had developed spastic quadriplegia, which caused his knees to lock in a sitting position with his feet pointed straight toward the floor and his toes curled under them like paper on a roll. His muscles contracted and become frozen that way. A spine made crooked by scoliosis caused him to hunch forward and to the side, so that a tray was put on his wheelchair to stop him from falling out of it.

Ray's face looked gaunt and haggard, with dark circles under his eyes as if he had been through hell. Still he managed a smile and a yelp of glee when he saw my mother. "Hi, Ray-Ray," I said to him. He looked in my direction, then turned his head down slightly and kept looking at me sideways. His eyes danced with laughter, and when he smiled his jaw slanted one way and his teeth slanted the other way. That crooked little smile captured my heart.

I knew that Ray didn't recognize me, but he smiled at anyone who gave him any attention. What a pleasant little man my brother was.

The plump caretaker patted Ray on the shoulder and said, "We're really concerned about Ray. We know he isn't feeling well when he won't eat. You know, Ray is our favorite. We all fight over who will feed him. He's always so smiley, and he never gives us a bit of trouble."

It was Ray's 50th birthday that day. His mind couldn't comprehend the milestone that he had reached against all odds. My mother gave Ray his birthday present. His one useful hand picked up the wrapped gift. Mom took it from him and unwrapped it to reveal a stuffed bear. He picked it up and threw it on the floor.

"Now, what kind of way is that to treat a gift?" Mom gently chided Ray. She didn't have far to reach to pick it up. Her petite body was shrinking with age. Mom gave the bear back to Ray and he dropped it on the floor again.

It dawned on me. "Mom, he wants you to play "dropsies" with him," I told her. She looked at me puzzled. "You know," I said, "that mindless game that kids love where they drop something and watch to see if you pick it up, time and time again, until you're so sick of it that you want to scream."

I found a cloth ball squished between Ray and the tray of his wheelchair. I tossed that with Ray to save wear and tear on his new teddy bear. Ray had quite a strong throw with his one fully functional hand. He actually perked up after I started playing with him, and I was blessed with his big, beautiful smile once again.

When I tired of throwing the ball, I just sat back and observed. Ray's arms were in constant motion. It was as if all of his energy was channeled into them. He was always grabbing at the thing closest to him. At that particular moment, it was the end of the strap on the seatbelt that kept him from falling out of his wheelchair. He was ignoring the necktie that was fastened to the arm of his chair.

I don't know what possessed me to do it, call it incessant curiosity; but I reached out to feel Raymond's legs. When I wrapped my fingers around his bare ankle, there was about a one-inch gap between my fingers and thumb. I jerked my arm back, bit my lip, and closed my eyes so my mother couldn't see the tears that welled up in them from the realization that Ray's legs had withered away to nothing from lack of use. Ray-Ray, what has become of you? I thought to myself.

"That's my Ray. He was always such a good boy," I heard Mom saying to another caretaker, when she came over to tell us what a pleasure it was taking care of Ray. He smiled all of the time. That smile was infectious.

My mom came over to Ray, and started telling me again what a beautiful baby he was. "Look at you, now," she cried. From then on I could see that it must have been hard for her when she put her little boy in a place so far away.

Mom confided in me again, "I wanted to keep Ray at home longer, but I had five kids, I was pregnant with your sister, and my father-in-law wanted to move in with us. I couldn't take care of all you kids, my father-in-law, and do everything for Ray, too. It was too much for me. It was too much for one person to handle."

While my mother was crying, Ray grabbed her hand and started patting it. That touching moment is etched in my memory forever. I was sorry that I hadn't spent more time with my gentle, loving brother. There were many times when I could have benefited from his gentleness and his enchanting smile. I vowed that I would never let many years pass before I came to see Ray again.

He was living in a much better place now. I could see that he was getting excellent care. But why was he so sick and why couldn't the doctors find out what was wrong with Ray?

Ray never did recuperate, and a feeding tube was placed into his abdomen to give him liquid nourishment. Afterwards he was placed into a different group home that took care of wards of the NYS DDSO who needed more medical attention. That was in the year 2001.

The group home was directly across from a small hospital. I visited Ray a few times at that home. It was just as welcoming as the last home Ray was in. The caretakers were just as kind and caring. We were invited to stop by anytime. They even offered to make us coffee and feed us as if we were part of their family.

Raymond had his feeding tube in for four years, and then it stopped functioning properly. They tried to take care of it at the hospital across from Ray's group home, but it was too complicated a task for the doctors there. The state, with the approval of my parents, decided that the best solution would be to send Ray to a larger hospital to be placed under the care of a team of gastroenterologists. That hospital was West End Community Hospital. It was actually closer to my parents' house than Ray's group home, so visiting Ray was easier.

My life has slowed down a bit, and I have had more time to follow my passion—writing. I now keep a journal of events that have profoundly changed my life. What happened to Ray next is one of them. The following is what took place after Raymond entered West End Community Hospital.

December 1, 2005 Thursday

I was talking to my mother on the phone today, and she said that Ray was still in the hospital. The poor thing, I had completely forgotten that he was supposed to go in. I was feeling like a negligent sister again. The guilt weighed heavily on me.

Ray was admitted on November 28. That was four days ago, and he is still there. They were going to take out the two tubes that he had going into his abdomen for feeding and replace them with one new tube. The procedure was only supposed to take a few days, and he was supposed to have been sent back to his group home. I feel so badly when he goes into the hospital because it's like putting a baby in a scary place, all alone.

I wanted to go see him, but the hospital he was in wasn't in a great part of town. They are taking great pains to build up that part of the city, but I still didn't feel safe going there alone in the dark.

I knew that if I had to get someone to come with me, I wouldn't be able to see Ray every day on my way home from work. A sinking feeling welled up in my stomach when I thought of Ray spending his nights at the hospital alone.

My dear husband, Mike, didn't hesitate at all when I asked him to accompany me to see Ray. We've been through hell together this year with the passing of his dad at home on October 23, after a short bout with pneumonia, and then the passing of his sister from a brain aneurism on November 9, just eighteen days later. Then five days later, a close cousin passed away. We were just coming out of the shock of those deaths when Raymond was admitted to West End Community Hospital.

The hospital parking ramp was one block away. The only person in the parking ramp was the man in the booth taking money. Mike and I walked to the hospital on deserted streets. I had been told that the hospital had security, but I saw absolutely no security personnel on the streets. I inched as close to Mike's big, burly body as I could get without tripping over him. I definitely won't be going to this hospital in the dark alone, I told myself.

The big lobby was welcoming, with soothing colors and comfy-looking, overstuffed chairs. We went to the reception desk and got our passes to get to Ray's floor from one of the three people manning the desk. We passed the security desk to get to the elevators. The security video camera was on, but there was no one at the desk to watch it.

We got off of the elevator on the surgical ward and walked the long hallway until we found Ray's room. Ray was all alone. There was another bed in the room, but it was unoccupied. His TV was off, so he was just lying there pulling on a necktie that was knotted to the railing of his bed. The tie was pretty ratty looking, so I knew that it had been the only thing keeping Ray occupied all day.

We were greeted with Ray's beaming smile. He just loved our attention. Who wouldn't when you're stuck in a room all alone for hours? Ray started rubbing his head with his hand like he was tired.

I could see that the side of his face was scratched. Ray must have done that to himself. I checked his fingernails. They were long and sharp at the corners. I looked around to see if there was a nail file or clippers, but there were none to be had.

I'm a nosy person, so I took off Ray's sheet and started checking him. He was lying on his side in a fetal position with his atrophied legs curled up underneath him. He wasn't able to sit up in bed or lie on his back because his legs and back could not be straightened out. The toes on his feet were bent every which way. When I had last seen him, he had socks on, so I didn't know if his toes were like that then. His back, which was twisted from scoliosis, seemed to have gotten worse since the last time I'd seen him.

Ray's bed was wet from urine and dark yellow ooze that was coming out from around the two tubes in his stomach. His stomach was beet red, and part of it looked crusty. I was shocked at his condition. I started to cry, but caught myself. I didn't want to cry in front of Ray. Instead, I went in search of someone who could change Ray's sheets. No one should be left in that condition.

The floor was eerily quiet. It shouldn't be like this, I thought to myself, especially on a surgical ward. I thought that people coming out of surgery were critical and needed to be checked regularly. I walked up and down the hall until I found a young black woman with her hair cropped to her scalp on one side and sweeping down to her chin on the other. Her bright orange scrubs were a welcome sight on an otherwise drab floor. "My brother's bed is a mess. Can someone come and change him?" I asked her.

"Okay, we'll be there," she said. She came a few minutes later with a thin man in his forties. He didn't appear to be all that brilliant, but what he lacked in the smarts category he made up for in compassion. While Mike and I were waiting in the hall, I heard him and the female aide talking affectionately to Ray as they were changing him. Ray doesn't like to be disturbed, so he was making a sort of half-growling, half-grumbling noise the entire time the aides were changing him. It was unnerving for me to hear it for the first time. When the aides came out, I thanked them. I knew that changing Ray wasn't a pleasant task.

Not too long after that, Ray started to doze off. Then the beeper on the monitor of Ray's IV pole went off. Beep! Beep! Beep! It was so annoying. I waited patiently to see if anyone came in. About ten minutes passed, and no one came. I looked out into the hall to see if anyone had noticed the beeping. No one was coming toward Ray's room. I went down the hall again and caught the attention of the aide in orange. "The beeper on my brother's IV is going off," I informed her. She came in and silenced it.

"The nurse should be in, soon," the aide said, as she made a hasty exit. The beeper went off again. Again I waited. Still no one came. I looked out into the hall. My eyes met the aide's. "Are you looking for the nurse?" she asked. I nodded yes. She pointed down the hall past me. I turned, and there was a nurse with a med cart about two rooms down.

The nurse noticed me looking at her. "I'll be there soon. I'm just doing 13 now," she said. I assumed that meant that she was working on a patient in room 1413. Ray's room was 1416. That was three rooms down. I waited another 20 minutes, and still she didn't come into Ray's room.

I was tired, so Mike and I left, but Ray's beeper was still going off as we made our way to the elevators. What do I know about beepers on IVs? No one seemed concerned, so I figured the beeper wasn't important. I knew that the nurse eventually was going to get there.

When I got home, it started nagging me. I didn't know what that beeper was for. If they let it go for more than 30 minutes without checking on Ray, what else are they ignoring? The whole time I was at the hospital, the only people that came into Ray's room were the aides, after I went and got them twice. I didn't have a good feeling about what I saw today.

December 6, Tuesday

My family doesn't know why Ray is still in the hospital. My parents are visiting Ray daily, but it's hard for them to find a doctor with whom they can speak. One never seems to be around when my parents are there. The group home is trying to get information by calling the nurses' station, but even they are having trouble getting anyone to tell them what exactly is happening with Ray.

Mike and I went down to see Ray again. This time the TV was on, but his bed was positioned so that he couldn't see it. The call button was on the bed beside Ray, as if he was going to figure out how to use it. There were surgical gloves and squares of gauze scattered about on the floor. I found a booklet from the group home giving information about Ray on the windowsill under a package of surgical pads. I know that no one has read it. Ray was still oozing yellow and green stuff from around the two tubes in his stomach. His IV was out. I went down the hallway and found a nurse to tell her about Ray's IV. She said that she would take care of it.

I had brought a small stuffed bear for Ray to play with. We played dropsies for awhile. Ray would pick up the bear and drop it by my hand. I'd pick it up and give it to him. He'd drop it again, and so on, until he got bored. Then I made the bear dance. That got a chuckle out of Ray. He must have been so bored being in bed all day by himself. I know that people from the group home stop in periodically, and Mom and Dad come every day, but still he is left alone for hours at a time.

Ray wet himself while Mike and I were there. I went in search of someone to change him. I've never seen a hospital floor as quiet as the one Ray was on. I walked up and down the deserted halls until I found the same aide who had changed Ray a few days ago. That nice male aide also came with her. Again, I could hear them talking gently to Ray while we waited in the hall. Again, I thanked them for changing him. Ray was such a mess.

Mike watched TV, while I thought of every antic that I could possibly do to entertain Ray. I sang. I made his stuffed bear fly. I made the bear dance. I hit Ray on the face with his tie. I made the bear kiss him. I made the bear kiss me. It was exhausting to entertain him, but so rewarding to see his smile.

I waited until Ray fell asleep, and still no one had come in to re-insert his IV. I left not sure if I should trust the nurse who said that she would take care of it. I knew that my parents would be in to see Ray tomorrow and would be checking on him, but how long can someone be without an IV before their body is harmed?

December 8, Thursday

Today they put a scope down Ray's throat into his abdomen to see if his tube was in place, or something like that. I'm still confused as to what they're trying to do with Ray. I'm getting frustrated with my mom. She can't seem to get any information from the nurses, the doctors, or the group home, and I can't understand why. "Sometimes, you have to be a pain in the butt and get in their faces until they get someone to talk to you," I admonished Mom. Doesn't she want to know what's going on with her son?

The ladies at my job now know about my brother because I've been talking to them about the treatment he's getting, or in his case not getting. One of my co-workers had a problem with a nurse at a different hospital when her mother was there. She advised me, "You should go down to the nurses' station and ask to speak to the nurse in charge that day and express your concerns." Okay, I was ready to do that today.

My youngest sister, Lynn, was going with me to see Ray today. She's my only sibling left in the area. My two brothers and older sister have all moved to other parts of the eastern United States.

I don't think I've ever had a fight with Lynn, even while growing up at our parents' house. I think we get along so well because we're so different. She's everything I'm not. She has curly auburn hair, perfect eyes, and a calm disposition. My poker-straight hair defies all grooming techniques. My eyes are bad, and my life is way too hectic. She's sugar and spice, and I'm spit and vinegar. I call Lynn the "good daughter." Me, well, I'm the "difficult daughter." I was born kicking and screaming. Time and physical maladies have mellowed me, but I still put up a good fight if riled enough.

Lynn and I have always tried to conquer difficult family situations together, so off the two of us went to see Ray and to give each other moral support.

Before Lynn and I made the trip, I called Ray's floor to make sure that he was back in his room after they did the scope thing. Yes, I was told, he had returned to his room.

When we got to Ray's room, it was pitch black. I thought that maybe he was sleeping off the anesthetic from his test, but when Lynn and I entered the room, Ray's sparkling eyes and radiant smile gleamed at us through the dark. I flicked on the light in his room to find a puddle of urine on the floor and his bed soaked, yet again. How long had he been left without anyone checking on him? Ray couldn't speak for himself, so he was being neglected.

Lynn left the room in search of someone to change Ray. I don't know what she said to them, but they came immediately. I didn't know what to do. I was so overwhelmed with emotions that I couldn't say or do anything at that moment. If I did react at that time it would have been to scream at I-don't-know-who or to wail at the neglect that my brother was enduring. I just stood in the hall while they were changing Ray and hid my crying from Lynn.

After Ray was all cleaned up, Lynn and I entered Ray's room again and went about trying to entertain him. We discovered that Raymond just loves the words "burp" and "fart." Let's face it, gaseous eruptions are funny when you have a boyish mind. Wouldn't it be a great world if everyone were so easily amused? We entertained Ray with fart and burp noises until he fell asleep.

As we were readying to leave, I put a kiss on my fingertips and touched it to the top of Ray's head. I woke him up. Darn. I hated leaving him when he was awake. I felt like Lynn and I were abandoning Ray.

I went to bed crying and begging Ray's angels to show me a way to help him when I can't be there. It's so cruel what's happening to Ray.

December 9, Friday

I made up my mind to call Ray's group home today and talk to someone who would care. Maybe they would give me an idea of what I could do to get better treatment for Ray. My brain was so overloaded with emotions that I couldn't think clearly.

I didn't get the name of the person at the group home with whom I spoke, but she told me to call the hospital and ask for the director of nurses. I called the main number of the hospital and asked to speak to the director of nurses, but they gave me the patient advocate.

"I have a brother who was admitted to your hospital who is mentally retarded and unable to speak for himself or even move by himself," I told her. "He's completely helpless. I've been in to visit him several times, and I'm very upset at the conditions I've been finding him in. The first time I went in, he was soaked in urine and I had to get someone to change him."

"Did you complain to the head nurse?" the patient advocate asked.

"No. I'm new to this," I replied. "I have to admit that I'm to blame also. I just assumed that the group home was making sure Ray was taken care of. Later that same night, his IV monitor was beeping . . . " I went on to explain what I had found the first and second nights, then the night Lynn and I found Ray in the dark with a puddle of urine on the floor. I continued, "Another time, I went in, and his IV was out. This is what I find when I do come in. I don't want to think of what happens to him on the nights I don't come in.

"Now, I talked to my parents and the people from his group home, and they come in during the day. They say that Ray seems to be taken care of all right during the day. I come in at night, and I'm telling you that it's scary. There seems to be hardly anyone working at night. Now, I have no complaints about his care when I do get someone to come and take care of Ray, but I can't be there every single night making sure that he's getting proper care. I understand that he's more difficult than most patients."

"No, that shouldn't be an excuse," the patient advocate replied. "Your brother should get better care than what you've described. I'm going to talk to the director of nursing, and she will address your concerns and call you; then she will follow up with a written report."

Being a writer, I always carry a pen and paper with me, so it was easy for me to keep track of dates and in what conditions I had found Ray. I started documenting everything after the second day, when I saw that Ray wasn't getting proper treatment. I pulled out my calendar and notes and gave my information to the patient advocate.

"Thank you so much," I said as I hung up the phone. I had found a sympathetic ear at the hospital. Now we'll see if she will keep her word.

After a little while, I got a call from my father. "The group home called me," he said. "They gave me the name of Ray's advocate. They asked me to call you and have you call her." I told my dad that I had spoken to the hospital's patient advocate. Apparently, when Ray went into the hospital, the state assigned an advocate to him who visits the hospital to make sure he's getting proper treatment. Her name is Jean Jeffors.

I called her and told her what condition I was finding Ray in. She also had assumed that he was okay because she only saw him during the day when there seemed to be more help. I've been told by a co-worker that if you want to check up on someone's care in a facility, go at different times during the day, and you'll see how each shift works. Apparently, the night shift is short-staffed at West End Community Hospital.

"I'll speak with the director of nursing myself," Jean informed me.

"Can you give me any information on my brother, or can you speak only to my parents?" I asked.

"What do you want to know?" she replied.

I asked, "Can you tell me why he's been in the hospital so long? He was only supposed to be in there a few days. He's been in there for almost two weeks."

"Well, he had a severe infection in his abdomen when he was brought in, and the skin in that area is excoriated [breaking down] from his stomach juices leaking out because the feeding tube isn't fitting properly. They are trying to clear up the infection, and he had two tubes that they are taking out and replacing with one tube," Jean explained.

Okay, that made sense. Why couldn't my parents or the group home get anyone at the hospital to tell them this? Or, why didn't the group home or my parents call this woman to get answers? This whole thing is so confusing, and it shouldn't be.

My emotions are raging. I'm angry. I'm sad. I feel helpless. I feel hopeless. I feel overwhelmed. I need help.

I called Mia of the employee's assistance program funded by my employer. She's helped me through tough times before. I called under the guise of asking for references for grief support groups for my brother-in-law and his family. She gave me some leads to contact for that information. Then I started telling her how I was doing—how many deaths have occurred in my family in such a short time period, how I feel badly about not being able to help, and how my brother was in the hospital being neglected. I started crying.

Mia advised me, "First of all, you have to take care of yourself. Your brother-in-law and his family will find their own way of dealing with grief. You *are* helping them by making phone calls. You know, if you ever need to just get away, you can come down and talk to me."

"I know, I know," my voice cracked into the phone. I had to hang up because I was crying so hard that I couldn't talk anymore.

Denise, the girl sitting at the work-station next to me, looked over and asked, "Are you all right?"

I plucked a tissue out of the box on my desk, blew my nose, and said, "No." I got up and started pacing. I didn't know if I should walk to the bathroom, which would take me past all of my co-workers, who would see me bawling, or just stay at my desk and cry as quietly as I could.

My co-workers who sit closest to me have all cried at one point or another this year. Between the four of us, there have been seven deaths of close relatives this year. I've dubbed our little area as "The Crying Corner." We've all shared our tissues and tragic stories. They wouldn't mind my occasional sniffling.

The rest of the day, I sat at my desk and wept off and on as quietly as I could. I'm going to have to bring another supply of tissues into work.

December 10, Saturday

It's amazing what a better night's sleep I get on the weekends. After a refreshing night's rest, I realized that I wasn't suffering from grief as much as I was suffering from feeling so helpless. My way of dealing with an upsetting situation is to do something to make it better, and Ray's situation was so out of control that I couldn't figure out how to fix it. Of course, I was still grieving the loss of my father-in-law and sister-in-law, but I wanted to help and couldn't find any meaningful way to do so. I have only so much time and so much emotional strength. I have to help Mike's side of the family once my brother was better.

As for my brother, I will just have to visit him as much as I can to make sure that the hospital is taking care of him the way they should be. At least I can make sure that he is clean, comfortable, and not left in the dark.

December 11, Sunday

I was going to stop at the hospital gift shop to get Ray a stuffed animal, but the shop was closed. He was lying in the dark again when I went into his room. The floor was deserted again, and no one came in to check on Ray in the hour and fifteen minutes that Mike and I were there, but he was clean, and his bed was turned so that he could watch TV. His feet were moved, and a pillow had been put under his legs so that he wouldn't get bed sores.

The stuffed Santa that he had yesterday was gone. The stuffed whale and bear that I brought in previously also had disappeared. They must have gone down to the laundry with Ray's dirty bed sheets. Ray was left with just his stupid necktie, which kept falling to the side of the bed beyond his reach. I could see that he wasn't the least bit interested in the barely audible program on his TV. It was some nightly news show. Don't these people understand that

Raymond has the mentality of a child? Mike turned the TV channel to one with cartoons.

Ray seemed agitated today. He kept rubbing the side of his face, pulling down his eyes, and opening his mouth to emit that half-growl, half-moan, which is his way of complaining.

I couldn't seem to make him smile. Then I remembered how he loved burp and fart noises. Ray would laugh every time I said the words "burp" or "fart." Mike knocked on something in the room, and Ray laughed at that, too. So, every time Ray started whimpering, Mike would knock on something or I would say "burp" or "fart." We had Ray laughing quite a bit. He seemed to take extra delight in Mike's saying "burp" or "fart," like it was some male-bonding thing going on. I can't imagine what our repertoire of noises sounded like out in the hallway.

I didn't want to leave Ray alone without any toys to hold onto. The only thing that I could find in the room was a box of 11"-by-12" wipes. These were on Ray's windowsill on top of the booklet that I had found the second day I visited Ray, the one with information on how he can't communicate, the one that had a list of all of his ailments. It was still under the same box of wipes. It was obvious that no one had taken the time to read it.

Whatever happened to compassion and caring in nursing? That has gone by the wayside here, as it has in other hospitals. Now nursing is a matter of providing only the essentials because the nursing staff just doesn't have the time anymore. There is not enough help on this floor at night to take care of a person who needs constant attention, like Ray.

I took an 11"-by-12" wipe and balled it up. I took another one and covered up the ball-shaped one to make a ghost. I found bandage tape and put it around the neck of the ghost. I found a pen in my purse and drew a smiley face on it, then gave the ghost to Ray to hold. He smiled at it. He's so easy to amuse. After that success, Mike and I became more creative. I took one wipe to make legs, then another one to make arms, then another one to make a body and a head. Mike taped it all together. I drew a face on that one, too. Not bad for improvising. At least Ray had something to look at besides bad programming on TV and four drab walls with informational posters that he can't read.

December 12, Monday

The nursing supervisor of West End Community Hospital called me at work today. She asked, "You called today to complain about the treatment your brother was getting?"

"No, I called on Friday," I replied.

She was perplexed. "Well, I just got an e-mail today," she said. Whatever, I thought. She continued, "I apologize for what happened to your brother. I talked to the staff on that floor, and we're going to do a better job. Normally, our criteria is to check a patient every four hours."

That concerned me, especially on a surgical floor, but I didn't respond. Isn't the first day following surgery a critical one? Every four hours just doesn't seem right for a person who just had surgery. However, I had to give credit where credit was due because I try my best to be honest in everything. "I don't have a criticism about the care he's getting when he is getting it. They are very compassionate with Ray, but I have to go looking for someone to take care of him every time I'm at the hospital. And it just seems like this happens on the night shift. My parents don't complain, nor does anyone from his group home, but that's during the day when there is more staff," I told her.

"I have written in Ray's chart to check him every hour now," she said. "He'll get better care from now on."

"I know he's harder to take care of because he can't do anything for himself," I said.

"That doesn't matter. What happened to him never should have," she replied. She's the second person who has affirmed my feelings about the lack of care that Ray was getting. I felt better after hearing that.

I called my parents to tell them that I spoke to the patient advocate. Mom answered the phone. My dad hardly ever picks up the phone. "I don't know, Pat," she said. "He always seems okay when I see him. I just can't seem to get any answers on what is happening to him. It's so hard to get to speak to his doctor. I haven't even seen the doctor yet. And the group home is asking me if I know what's going on."

I told her what Ray's advocate, Jean Jeffors, said to me. "Mom, why doesn't the group home just call her? They're the ones who gave me her phone number. Why don't they call her?"

"I don't know, Pat." She sounded aggravated with me. What was I doing wrong? All I was doing was asking questions.

December 13, Tuesday

Jean Jeffors called me at the end of my work day. "I told you I'd call, so I'm giving you an update," she said.

I informed her, "The head of the nurses called me yesterday and apologized for what happened to Ray."

"Did she? That's good. We have to take care of Ray," she said.

"She said it's in his chart that he be checked every hour. Why isn't that put in the chart of every person like Ray as soon as he enters the hospital?" I asked.

"They normally don't just write something like that in a chart," she told me. "They should just automatically check people."

"But only every four hours?" I asked. "That's what the head of nursing said was their criteria." I got no answer to that question. "Why don't they put diapers on Ray so he doesn't lie in his own urine? That can't be good for his stomach to lie in urine."

"It's not their policy to put people in diapers. Besides, then they'd be checking on Ray less often. We don't want that. Do you want an update?" she asked.

"Sure," I replied.

"Well, they took out one of Ray's tubes. They're going to let that hole heal. The rash on his side is getting better. It still looks bad, but it's getting better," she said. She sounded so confident that Ray was improving. I believed her. Oh, how I wanted to believe her.

I thought everything was going to go smoothly. My prayers were being answered.

I got home from work and did what had become my routine for the past two weeks. I made my lunch, got together my clothes for work the next day, read my notes to myself reminding me what I had to do, ate supper, and made my way to the hospital with Mike.

When we got to Ray's room, he was completely naked, with his back facing the open door. I went up to his bed, and he grinned from ear to ear like he was delighting in having no clothes on. At first, I was upset. What was Ray doing in bed, entirely naked, with no blankets on, in the middle of winter? Then I found his gown squashed up on the side of the bed with his hands still in the sleeves. He must have pulled it off himself. He's always grabbing at things within reach of his hands. Anything cloth or stuffed like a toy was fair game with him. He must have gotten a hold of his gown. "Ray, what are you doing in bed naked? Are you trying to show off for your girlfriends?" He laughed at that. He reminded me of my son who, when he was a baby, took great delight in running around the house naked when I took off his diaper.

We weren't in Ray's room for long before his nurse for the night shift came in. Every night I've visited Ray, he's had a different nurse. At least the ones I have seen are different. She began, "Hello, Mr. Scawoo...Mr. Swar..."

"His name is Raymond. It's Raymond, and he can't talk," I said. I wanted to tell her to read the chart before she works on patients. "He has the mentality of a baby."

She tried to get him to do things on command. "He doesn't respond to commands. He needs someone to do everything for him," I told her. Read the chart. Doesn't it have Raymond's history in it? I wanted to yell at her.

"Oh," she said. She turned to me with this stupid, blank look in her eyes, and smiled. I thought, Oh, my God, I'm supposed to have faith that he's going to get better care from now on?

I left Ray's room, crying. Now it was Mike's turn to do the comforting. I had consoled him through the death of his father and sister, and now he had his arm around me as I cried in the lonely halls of West End. I don't know how we could have gotten through these months if we hadn't supported each other.

When I went to bed, I couldn't stop myself from imagining Ray all alone in the dark being ignored. I had to block that thought from my mind to keep my sanity because there was nothing that I could do about it. I tried talking to people. I complained to the patient advocate. I tried reasoning with people, and little had changed. At least Ray wasn't lying in his own urine anymore, but really, nothing had changed. I truly believe that the only hope of him getting better treatment is to get him back to his group home.

December 14, Wednesday

When I got to Ray's room today, a nurse was trying to get blood from him. It's hard to do that because his hands are in constant motion, except when he's sleeping. I could see that she was having trouble. He already had a swatch of gauze with a fresh blood stain taped further up his arm. I offered to help by holding his hands, but she still couldn't get any blood. "I'll have to send up someone else," she told me.

Poor Ray, his arms are black and blue from being poked with so many needles. He's probably getting dehydrated because he's not getting proper nutrition and hydration through the tubes in his stomach. With less fluid going through Ray's veins, it's even harder to draw blood.

Ray's poor lips are always cracked. He isn't getting any liquids through his mouth to moisten them. I, now, carry Vaseline in my purse and put it on Ray's lips every time I visit him. It must feel good to him because he rubs his lips together after I put it on. Simple things like that to make Ray feel more comfortable—the nurses don't seem to have time to do them. Vaseline once a day on the lips—how much time would that take?

I had to keep pulling Ray's gown and his blanket from his hands. He's always grabbing things like a little kid. I see that he has a yellow bear added to his little collection of critters. His stuffed Santa showed up again, along with the first bear that I had given him.

When I was out in the hall, while Ray was being changed, the male aide came up to me and told me, "I went down to the laundry one day when Ray didn't have any stuffed animals, and I couldn't find any of his, so I went to the gift shop and bought that yellow bear for him." There are still little pockets of compassion in this place. Ray seems to bring that out in people.

Later, a nurse caught me dancing for Ray with one of his stuffed animals. She laughed at me, then looked at Ray. "Hi buddy," she called to him. "He was smiling more yesterday," she said to me.

"Really? He was crying yesterday when I left," I said. He had real tears coming down his face then. I hate to see him cry. Today he was crying again when I left, but not as badly as yesterday. I wish I could stay with him overnight, but I couldn't possibly do that and keep my job. It's just tearing at my sensitive soul to see him like this.

December 16, Friday

Yesterday there was an ice storm. Today there was another winter storm-watch. People have been complaining about the bad weather for days, but I barely notice it. There's little that bothers me these days. All minor irritations are washed away by my tears.

My co-workers and I were watching the weather through the window at work and getting updates from our spouses from various locations north and south of the city. One minute, I looked out of the window, and the sun was shining. A few minutes later, it was dark and blustery. Then the wind stopped, and it started to snow lightly. The terrible storm predicted never did come to my neck of the woods.

Our office Christmas party was today. I was in the bathroom with one of my co-workers, and she asked if I was going to the party this afternoon. "No, I'm having a rough time this year, and I just don't feel like going out and celebrating," I replied. I didn't want to get into everything with her. I'd start bawling, and I had myself under control today.

"I'm sorry," is all she said. Really, how do you respond to what I just said?

Tonight, Mike and I did something fun. It's been about three weeks since we've been out amongst friends. Tonight, we worked the "Rockin' with Santa" Christmas toy collection drive. Admittance to see three bands play for free was a donated toy.

With the weather so bad, the turnout was disappointing, but those who attended had a great time. We danced and drank and collected toys. At times, I talked to my two friends about Ray and the hard time that I was having with getting him taken care of at the hospital. Everyone I talk to shakes their head in disbelief at what's happening to Ray, so I know that I'm not just being a nag when I complain about his treatment.

John, who put together the whole event, was getting anxious about the lack of people coming in because of the bad weather. I tried to reassure him. "Have faith. Just pray to God and have faith," I told him. "Do the best you can, and it'll all work out."

That's exactly what happened. There were so many donations and toys collected ahead of time that they wound up with more than last year's total. "You were right, Pat," John came up to tell me later. God works in mysterious ways, doesn't He? I wish I knew how God's mysterious ways were going to work with Raymond. Right now, I need to take my own advice and have faith that all will work out in the end.

Mike and I were home by 11:00 PM. We had to get up at 7:00 in the morning to sort out the toys so that the needy families sent to us from the St. Vincent De Paul Society could come and pick them up. I can't wait to see the looks on their faces when they see all that their kids would get. It's good for me to get away from my agonizing life and to help someone else who is also going through hard times.

December 19, Monday

My brother from Georgia called me at work and asked me to give him some ideas on what to buy Mom and Dad for Christmas. I don't know how he gets his Christmas shopping done. He certainly doesn't get stressed out at this time of year. More people should be like him.

Actually, this year I *am* more like him. I read on a grief support group's web site that you shouldn't make too much of the holiday season. Try not to make it the same as when your loved one was alive, because you'll fail. Whatever you decide to do, don't feel guilty about it. So, I'm not going to feel guilty about giving out lots of money and gift cards because I wasn't in the mood to shop.

I gave my brother some ideas, and we said our goodbyes. Then my mother called. She informed me, "I talked to Ray's doctor today. He said that he put two different tubes in, and the last one is still leaking. He's talking about taking the tube out and allowing Ray's holes in his stomach to heal and feeding him through an IV."

"Will he get enough nutrition that way?" I asked.

"I don't know. Dr. Rogue, his name was, said he'll talk to two other doctors, and they'll make their decision. There are just too many people taking care of Ray. He said he never saw anyone with two tubes in the same place. Ray won't be out of the hospital before Christmas," she said.

"Is that what the doctor said?" I asked.

"No, that's just how I feel," she replied. My mom, why was she so pessimistic? "I guess he's been carrying on these past few days."

"Well, he's sick of being there," I said.

"I know. I know," she said. "The nurse said he had been acting up. I asked if she gave him any pain medication."

Not only were they taking their dear, sweet time figuring out what to do with Ray, but now I fear they're drugging him up because he was getting antsy from being there for three weeks. They should put themselves in Ray's place. Wouldn't they be getting antsy if they were in Ray's condition and in the hospital for three weeks? I wish he could talk. Would they be treating a child who could talk like Ray was being treated?

"Dr. Rogue was asking all kinds of questions about Ray. Any doctor who treats Ray is always interested in him," my mother continued. Yeah, not interested enough to find out what to do with Ray, I wanted to tell her, but I held my tongue long enough to finish the conversation and hang up. My tongue is getting so sore from biting it to control my outbursts.

My mother is from the generation that trusts all doctors. I, on the other hand, question everyone and everything. It's my nature. My curiosity has prompted a few doctors to suggest that I seek treatment elsewhere, but at least I have more control over my health.

When I finished my conversation with my mother, I put my head in my hands and rested my elbows on my desk at work. I sat that way for a few minutes to compose myself. I'm so tired of this mess.

I went with Mike to see Ray tonight. I found a drugged-up, crippled-up, 54-year-old with an IV in his right arm near the elbow. That arm was swelled up to twice its size. The IV was dripping down Ray's arm onto his bed, apparently for some time, because his bed was soaked where his arm lay. How long does it take for something like this to happen? When was the last time he was checked? His stomach was oozing green all over his left side. It was gross, but I had to check to see how much was leaking. I wanted to see if I needed to point out that Ray needed cleaning up when I told the nurse about his IV.

Poor Ray. He had bruises from his hand all the way up his arm from being stuck with needles so many times. He kept lifting his right arm up then bringing it down on his head. He was pulling at his ear and rubbing his face. It was obvious that he was suffering by the grimace on his face. His pathetic little whimpering started me crying.

It wasn't long before a nurse and orderly came into Ray's room. *Now* when they see me on the floor, they come in right away. "His bed is all wet on this side," I said. I pointed to the side of the bed where Ray's IV was leaking. This is something you would notice if you checked on your patient, I wanted to say to her, but I held my tongue.

"He's still leaking from his abdomen," she told me as if to explain why she was ignoring her patient.

"No, this isn't on that side," I replied. I pointed to his arm. "His bed is all wet near his IV. It's leaking down his arm."

"It's indurated," she said. [The tissues in Ray's arm were getting hard because the IV fluid was leaking into them instead of going into his vein.] "That's the second time it's happened today," she continued. If it happened once, wouldn't you be checking to see if it happens again? Why am I always pointing out things that the nurses should be noticing? "I'm going to send in your buddy, Ray," the nurse told us. She meant the aide in the orange fatigues.

In a few minutes, the nurse came back with the aide, the only staff besides the male orderly that I see on a regular basis. "What's up, Ray?" the aide asked.

"He's not doing so well today," I informed her. She lifted up Ray's sheets and saw that he needed changing.

Mike and I went outside into the hall while they cleaned Ray up. "He's lost his oomph," I said.

"I know, he's hardly growling," Mike replied. Poor Ray, his energy was slowly being sapped out of him.

"I don't know why he's still alive," I said. I meant that in two ways. He had lost so much weight and been through so much. Most people would have died by now. I also wondered why God was keeping him alive for so long. I told God that whatever Ray was put on earth to do, he must have done it by now. He could take him back now and stop his suffering. The poor thing, he's nothing but skin and bones. He was like that before he came to the hospital, but now he's even worse. I thought that the Hippocratic oath for doctors stated first to do no harm. I can't see how Ray's better off than he was before he came to West End. He's only getting worse.

"You can come in, now," the nurse said. I saw that she had taken out the IV. That may have been why Ray had been holding up his arm, because it was bothering him. Now he had stopped lifting his arm and wasn't whimpering anymore.

The nurse said, "Personally, I think that Ray's abdomen should be packed more. But the doctor doesn't think so. That can't be good, that stuff leaking all over his stomach." I knew that she wanted me to see that she cared about Ray. If she really cared, she would have been checking on him more often and seen that his arm was swelling up.

I tried cutting Ray's fingernails. He's been scratching his face again because they're still long and sharp. If I want the hospital personnel to cut them, they have to have the doctor write up an order for a podiatrist to do it. I could only get two nails cut because Ray kept yanking his hand away. He had to have it constantly moving.

"Ray-Ray, I wish I could help you," I told him. I patted his hand, unable to think of anything else to do. Ray wasn't in the mood for entertaining with my stupid antics. After about an hour, Mike came and stood on the other side of Ray's bed. Ray reached over, grabbed Mike's jacket, and smiled weakly. Ray was male-bonding with Mike again. "You get Mike. He's your buddy, isn't he?" I said. For a few minutes, Ray hung onto Mike and smiled in between whimpering.

Ray finally dozed off, and I snuck in some nail clipping and filing while he slept peacefully. I planted a kiss on my hand, touched it to Ray's face, and bid him a tearful goodbye. I can't stand to see helpless people suffering.

Later, I talked to Lynn to see when she was coming over to bake cookies. She had taken Mom to see Ray on Sunday. He was crying and moaning so much that Mom convinced the nurses that Ray needed pain medication. His chart was checked, and they were told that none was ordered. How can that be? A person in his state and no pain meds were ordered, not even on an as-needed basis? I don't understand. How can you look at him and not put that in his chart? And I don't understand how doctors can allow someone in Ray's state to continue on for three weeks in obvious discomfort and still not come up with a definitive plan of action.

Lynn said that Mom asked her if the doctors couldn't get the feeding tube to work, would she think her mother was cruel if she decided to take Ray off of everything and just let him die? After seeing Ray today, I have to say that it would be more cruel to keep him alive. I don't know how I'll be able to handle another death this year.

I prayed to Ray's angels not to let him suffer any longer. Then I cried myself to sleep again.

December 20, Tuesday

I was so weepy today I had to keep going to the bathroom so people wouldn't look at me weirdly and ask why I'm crying during this beautiful holiday season.

I cried. Then I left a message on the voice mail of Ray's advocate. I waited for her to call back. Then I cried some more. I tried to keep my mind on other things, like my work, so I wouldn't weep all day.

My heartbeat is irregular. This happens to me sometimes when I'm tired or stressed out, but it has been so constant lately that I'm afraid I'll have to go back to my heart specialist and be put on medication again. The last time that happened, the meds made me so sick with diarrhea that I made the doctor take me off of them. If I can just have a month or even one week without stress, I can get better.

I think I'm suffering from post-, present- and future-traumatic stress disorder. The exhaustion is overwhelming. I have no energy for the holidays. I really wish that they would just pass me over. I don't know how I'm going to cook Christmas dinner for my family.

I called Mom to tell her the state that I found Ray in yesterday. She wasn't going to see him today. She said that she was tired. When I told her that someone other than me needs to complain about his treatment, she responded with, "I do complain, Pat. I complain to the nurses."

"Mom, nurses can't change anything. It's the doctors who write the orders," I said.

"He has so many doctors," she replied. "I don't think any of them know what to do with Ray."

"Well, then someone has to complain to the administration of the hospital," I said.

"I'm sorry, I don't know what to do. I called the group home and told them Ray won't be home for Christmas.

"And?" I said.

"Well," she replied, "the doctor said that he was going to take the tube out."

"Mom, they said they were going to take it out yesterday, and they didn't," I said.

"I know," she replied. "They told me two different times that they were going to take it out."

"And they didn't; they didn't, Mom," I said.

"Well," she told me, "I'll go down tomorrow and see if they take it out."

"I called Ray's advocate," I said. "She told me everything that was going on with Ray the last time. I left a message for her to call me back."

"Well, I'll go down to see him tomorrow and see what's happening," my mom finished. With that, she hung up.

I was so upset when I hung up the phone. I just get so irritated that nothing is being done for Ray. No one has answers. Why does he lie in the hospital all alone, day after day, wallowing in his own body fluids, without anyone knowing what's going on? Isn't his group home supposed to be making sure that he's taken care of? Why aren't they doing anything? Why am I the only one who seems to be fighting for Ray? I have so many unanswered questions swirling around in my head, and it's making me dizzy.

When Lynn came to my house after dinner to bake Christmas cookies, I told her of my conversation with Mom. "Lynn, she wasn't going to see Ray today," I told her.

"Well, I know it exhausts her," Lynn said.

"But he's in the hospital alone." I told her. A picture of Ray all alone in the hospital kept popping into my head.

Lynn has a way of calming me down. Maybe it's just her demeanor, but it wasn't long before I relaxed and we got into making cookies. At night's end, we traded cookies. We each wound up with four different kinds. Just what I need, more comfort food that I can shove in my face to add pounds to my ever-growing behind.

I couldn't sleep again. When I close my eyes at night, I get a sinking feeling in the pit of my stomach. I can feel Raymond's fear — the fright of a sick child left alone in a room at the furthest end of the hospital ward for weeks. It's the same gripping fear I felt as a child when my parents sent me to bed, well before my siblings, to sleep in a dark room in the furthest corner of the house from where the rest of my family was. I'd breathe as quietly as I could so the demons of the night wouldn't notice me cowering under my covers. Little old me would never have been able to fight them alone. I understand Raymond. I understand.

December 21, Wednesday

I was at work and couldn't concentrate again, so I looked through the phone book for malpractice attorneys. There were pages and pages of them. I ripped out a few pages and put them in my purse. I think we have a good case for a neglect suit, but I doubt that my parents would want to sue. They're already going through enough.

I called my mother to see if she was going to see Ray, and if she could get answers as to why Ray was in the hospital for so long. "Pat, you don't understand, one person tells me one thing, then another person tells me something else. I've *been* trying," she told me.

"Well, you have to ask questions. You have to get in their faces, Mom, until they tell you what you want to know," I said.

"Pat, I *am* trying," she replied. I know I was being harsh with Mom, but we needed to get answers, and no one else in our family can go to the hospital during the day to talk to the doctors. Someone else needed to get information. I needed her help. I couldn't do it by myself.

I hung up the phone, and figured I'd take matters into my own hands. I called the hospital's patient advocate. "Susan, you remember me, Raymond — — — —'s sister?" I asked her.

"Yes, I do," she replied.

"My family is trying to get answers on just what is happening to Ray. They say each time they talk to a doctor, if they can even get to talk to one, they get different stories. Can you give me any advice on what to do to get information?" I asked.

"You should go to the nurses' station, ask to speak to the head nurse, and have that nurse set up an appointment to meet with the coordinating doctor," she said.

"Okay. My brother has been getting better treatment since my first complaint, and I thank you for that," I told her.

"I remember, you said that your parents were getting older and may be getting confused. While you're there, you might want to have them sign a release to allow the hospital to give you information on Ray," she said.

My mom said that she and my dad were going down to see Ray today, so I called her back. I'm thankful that I have an understanding supervisor who doesn't mind my making so many calls during working hours. I told her what the patient advocate said to do to be able to talk to Ray's doctor; not some intern, but the doctor who is supposed to be coordinating his care. This Dr. McDougal, who is supposed to be coordinating Ray's care, never seems to be available, but the hospital's patient advocate said that we could make an appointment with him.

I asked my supervisor for permission to leave work early. Then I called Mom again to say that I got permission to leave work to be with her and Dad when they went to the nurses' station. A few minutes later, I called her again because the weather was getting bad and asked her if she wanted me to pick her up. She said no. I think she was getting perturbed with me. "Okay, I won't call again," I said jokingly. Was I being too pushy? At that point, I didn't care. I just wanted answers and so did my parents, and this was the only way I could think of to get them.

The snow was falling heavily when I got out of work. I drove from work to the hospital right through the bad part of town. I got near the parking garage and put on my brakes to slow down and turn in, but I just kept on going right past the entrance. Around the block I went for another try. Again I skidded right past the entrance. Once more, around the block I went. This time I started slowing down a full block before the entrance. At last, I made it. Try and try again is my motto. I wish that would work where my brother was concerned.

I met my parents in Ray's room. Then we went down to the nurses' station together. What a chaotic place that was with nurses and aides coming and going and doctors walking about. It's not like that at night. Once someone noticed us, we asked to make an appointment to speak with Ray's doctor, the one coordinating Ray's care. Ray's nurse for the day said, "That would be Dr. Dansk." That wasn't the name my parents were given when Ray was admitted, but I wrote it down and asked for the spelling.

My dad asked, "What is that for? In case we have to go to court?"

"I don't know. I'm just keeping track. In this place you have to do things like this," I replied. As we were standing at the desk, a woman came out of a room across the hall. Her name badge said "Jill." I wrote that name down, too.

"Are you Raymond ———'s family?" she asked. "I heard you saying his name. I'm working on his release. His group home agreed to take him back. He should be released soon. I paged the doctor for you. You should go back to Ray's room and wait there."

Then Dr. Rogue walked by. My mother stopped him, "Dr. Rogue?" she asked.

"I'm not a doctor," he said.

"Oh," she said, "we're trying to get answers about Ray and what is going on with him."

"Let me take down your phone number, and I'll talk to his doctor and call you tomorrow," he said. I knew that he probably wouldn't.

We went back to the room and waited patiently. We waited for two hours, and still no doctor came. Raymond's lips were so cracked that they were bleeding into his mouth. Today he had a urine catheter in. He was so dehydrated that the urine in his catheter bag was orange, and his IV was out, yet again. That was the third time I found him with his IV out. This time, they put it in the top of his hand and secured it with a tiny piece of tape. How was that supposed to stay in when his hands were in constant motion?

I pointed it out to Ray's male nurse. He just shook his head. He had to page someone from a different department to come to re-insert it. He kept rushing up and down the hall, and occasionally he would poke his head into the room. "The doctor still isn't here? They still didn't come in to put in a new IV?" he asked. I knew he cared but had little control over a doctor or the IV team.

After 2½ hours, the doctor came in. She was a slight woman who spoke with a Slavic accent, not the Dr. McDougal whom we were told was overseeing Ray's care. Why is he so elusive? Does he even exist? I thought. Dr. Dansk's auburn hair bobbed as she slowly and patiently explained everything they had done to Ray while he was in that hospital.

He had come in with an infected abdomen, which they had tried to clear up, she told us. He also had a fissure inside his abdomen. They didn't want to just take out the tubes in Ray's stomach and close up the holes before the fissure healed, because it would leak into the abdomen. So, I wondered, leaking onto his skin was better? I didn't get to ask the doctor that question because I was concentrating so hard to understand her heavy accent over Ray's growling in the background.

The doctors had tried several tubes, she continued, which hadn't worked. They were hoping that the current one would function properly. The last resort would be to put in a PICC (Peripherally Inserted Central Catheter) line and feed him through that. They didn't want to do that because there is a great chance of infection and other complications with it, not to mention that it would be artificial nutrition that wouldn't be absorbed as well as liquid nutrition by the body through the abdomen. Once her lengthy explanation was over, she rushed out of the room. She was in the final hours of her 27-hour shift. That hospital was scary.

Dad motioned me to come over to where he sat. "Now, say that all over again, please," he said. "I didn't hear a word that she said." It's a good thing that I was in the room with my parents, because I had to repeat everything to Mom, too.

After repeating all the details to Mom and Dad, I shook my head. "Now I know why you get so confused when you're trying to get information. This place is so chaotic," I told them.

I went home and called Ray's advocate. She had never returned my call of a few days earlier. Her voice mail came on. I said, "I just wanted to tell you what condition I found Ray in today. His lips were dry and so cracked that they were bleeding into his mouth. He's so dehydrated that his urine is orange, and his IV was out, yet again." With that, I hung up. Let her deal with that.

December 22, Thursday

After work today, I had an appointment with my general practitioner for a wellness physical. His assistant weighed me in and took my blood pressure. I had gained ten pounds, and my blood pressure was 152-over-something. The stress is getting to me. When the doctor came into the room, he began by reviewing my blood tests. "Your sugar levels are great, and your cholesterol levels are great," he said.

Before he could say anything more, I jumped in, "Now you're going to yell at me about my weight and blood pressure, but before you do, let me tell you about what I've been through the past three months." I went through all the family deaths and what was happening to Ray.

"Well, I guess you have been through a lot," he said. "I know the chief of surgeons at West End. If you still have problems, give me a call and maybe I can be of help." There are compassionate people all over who want to help Ray and my family.

My doctor took my blood pressure again at the end of our visit, and it had gone down to 132-over-something. "Maybe all you needed was to do a little venting," he assured me. Oh, I needed to vent, all right. I needed to do a lot of venting, but there were too many people involved. I didn't have time or energy enough to vent at them all.

I went home, had dinner, and went once more to see Ray with Lynn. By now, the people at the desk in the lobby handing out the passes know our faces and remember Ray's last name. "Is he still here?" the elderly woman at the desk asked. I bit my tongue and just nodded in response.

Ray's eyes were droopy like he was doped up, and there were mitts on his hands because the nurses say he keeps pulling out his IVs. He's not purposely pulling them out. He doesn't pay any attention to them when I'm with him. They just don't know how to put one in so it will stay on someone who is constantly moving his arms. The first IV Ray had was in for at least a week because they wrapped gauze over it after they put it in. They just don't know how to take care of a special-needs person at West End.

Ray kept looking at his hands. They had cut off his lifeline. His hands were the only thing on his body that still functioned, and he couldn't use them if they were covered up. He didn't want those mitts on, and I couldn't blame him. I feel a lot of people have a hard time seeing Raymond as a normal person. He has the same feelings as any human being. Why can't people see that? Oh, how I wish he could talk so that he could complain to the nurses about those mitts on his hands.

The nurse that came into Ray's room tonight said that Ray was being discharged tomorrow. I asked her if she knew when. She gave me the phone number of the nurses' station and said that the doctors make their rounds in the early morning at 5:00. "So, if I call around 9:00 in the morning, we'll know when he'll be sprung?" I asked. I wanted to get my facts straight because, well, you can see that the hospital was not good at getting things right. Lynn could corroborate my information.

Lynn and I left Ray around 9:15 PM, after he had dozed off peacefully. When we got to the lobby, it was empty: no security, absolutely no one. We tried going down the hallway and out the side door that we had come in earlier. It was locked. We tried to get back through the doors in the hallway to get back into the lobby, but they had closed behind us. Now we were stuck between two sets of doors. Lynn finally yanked hard on the doors so that we could get back into the lobby, and there was a woman sitting in a chair by the front doors who hadn't been there before. "You have to go out there," she said, pointing to revolving doors.

Why weren't there signs or security to show us the way out? And where was security? My anxiety level peaks every time I visit that hospital.

When I got home, I wrote in my journal. I feel compelled to tell Ray's story. Maybe if I do, people like him will get better treatment when they're hospitalized.

December 23, Friday

I had off today, but I couldn't sleep in. My body is in constant stress mode. Even though I know that Ray is going home today, I'm so upset by what's happened to him that it occupies my mind all of the time.

I called the nursing station as planned at 9:00 AM. "Can you tell me when my brother Raymond — — — is being discharged today?" I asked.

"Let me see," the nurse replied, "Raymond — — —." She said it like she's never heard of that name before. He's been on your floor for four freaking weeks! I wanted to shout into the phone. There was silence for a few minutes. Then she finally said, "There are no discharge papers in his chart."

"What do I have to do to get my brother out of there?" I asked.

"I'll page Dr. Dansk," she said.

As I waited, I tapped my foot. That's how I maintain control when I'm angry. I release my anger through an appendage by striking something inanimate, so that my anger isn't released on the person at whom I want to explode. In a few minutes, Dr. Dansk was on the phone. I complained to her, "I was told that my brother is being released today. I called the nurses' station, and they say that there are no release papers in his chart."

"I don't understand. I signed all of those papers yesterday," the doctor said. "Yes, he's going to be released today. They just have to…" she went on with some unfamiliar terminology about his feeding tube. "That should be done about 11:00 this morning," she finished.

Great, Ray was going to be getting out of that place. Something told me to call the group home, because they were the ones who had to come and get him. No, I found out, they hadn't been called. Now, you think that if they had a 45-minute drive to the hospital, they would have been called well ahead of time. "I'm having Jill Tillman [a patient release coordinator] paged," the person at the group home said.

So, that was her full name. I tried calling her yesterday, but didn't know her last name. I had known her only as "Jill," who coordinated the release of patients on the surgical floor. After being transferred around at least three times, I had been told that no one by that name worked at that hospital.

"Well, I was told that he was being released at 11:00, so I'll just go up there about 10:30 and make sure he gets released," I said. I didn't have a good feeling about this.

I called my mother as a courtesy to tell her that I was going up to the hospital to find out what was going on with Ray's release. "You're kidding. I was just going to go shopping," she said. I was planning to go by myself, but she decided to come with me. "There's more leverage if Ray's mother is there," Mom said. I doubted that, but I humored her.

I called Lynn's house. I left a message on her voice mail. "I'm leaving a message because you have caller ID, and you'd know it was me, and if I just hung up you'd worry something is wrong. I'm letting you know that I'm going to the hospital to spring Ray today. I just wanted to tell you in case they lock me up in the mental ward there or take me away to the police station," I finished. I was getting punchy from all the stress and exhaustion.

Once I had picked up my mother, I headed off to the hospital again. I can't tell you the complete, utter exhaustion that I feel. I'm so tired that I don't even notice the Christmas decorations all around me. When asked what I'm doing for Christmas, I first have to stop and focus my brain so that I can fathom what time of year it is. Then I have to say, "I'm sorry, I haven't thought much about it." After that response, people look at me like they're wondering what planet I've been on.

On the way to the hospital, Mom was talking about getting Ray back to the group home. "They're such nice people there," she said.

At that time I was upset with them because I had found out yesterday that the group home could have made arrangements for someone to be with Ray at the hospital. I had talked to a co-worker who had a developmentally disabled brother in a group home also run by the NYS DDSO. The brother fell and broke his leg. He had to be hospitalized, and that group home made arrangements to have a person from Firstcare Inc. come to stay with him, feed him, and help care for him the whole time that he was there. Firstcare is a temporary agency that specializes in health care.

After I was told that, I had called Ray's group home and spoke to an aide who corroborated my co-worker's story. She tried to placate me by saying, "Sometimes the people from Firstcare are good. Sometimes they're bad. I've heard of one person who left her patients alone for hours. I don't know where she went, but she wasn't in her patient's room."

I then talked to a friend who works at a local group home also run by the NYS DDSO. She said the same thing. The family can request it. Well, what if the family doesn't know they can? Does it just not get done?

"Mom, I don't care if they're nice at Ray's group home," I told her. "Nice gets you nothing. I don't care if they are the biggest jerks in the world, as long as they're taking good care of Ray. Why didn't they have someone come to stay with Ray, especially after I told them what condition I was finding him in? I spoke to some of the people from the home, and they told me that when they came to see Ray at the hospital, they also had to go find nurses to change him."

I was fit to be tied between finding that out and this mix-up with Ray's release. I knew that I was being short with my mother, but I was too tired to try to be nice. My wrath was being directed at her again.

The elevator doors opened on Ray's floor. We got off and first went to see Ray. He was in his wheelchair, complaining. He still had those stupid mitts on his hands. How would you feel if you had gloves on for two days? I'd be complaining, too. I looked at Mom and said, "Are you ready?" We walked down to the nurses' station and planted ourselves in front of it until someone noticed us.

The nurse behind the counter asked, "Can we help you?"

"My brother, Raymond — — —, is supposed to be released today," I said.

After a few minutes of checking in Ray's chart, the nurse looked up at us and said, "We have no discharge papers for Raymond." Well, that just sent me over the brink.

I told her, "I can't believe this place. This is ridiculous. I spoke to Dr. Dansk at 9:00 this morning, and she said that he would be released by 11:00 today. A Jill Tillman said that she was working on his release, and the nurse said last night that he was definitely going home today! This place is so screwed up..."

"Unfortunately Jill isn't in today," the nurse said.

"Yeah, well I tried talking to her yesterday and was told she doesn't even work here. I'd like to speak to Dr. Dansk who said that Ray was being released," I said.

"I'll have to page her," she replied. I paced back and forth and back and forth, ranting in front of the nurse's station. "Will you please wait in Raymond's room, and the head nurse will come in to talk to you there?" she asked. Now they were trying to get me away from the nurse's station so that I didn't upset the patients and their families.

My mother, whom I didn't hear say a thing probably because of my ranting, came back to Ray's room with me. I sat on his bed. A few minutes later, a nurse came in with an attitude. "I don't know why you're so upset with us. It's Ray's group home that won't take him back," she said.

"Why were we told that they would? Jill told us that they agreed to take him," I countered. There were no conditions mentioned. She just said that they had agreed to take him. I'm a reasonable person. If I was told that Ray would be released under certain conditions, I wouldn't have been upset. West End needs to improve their communication skills.

The nurse said, "Well, they won't take him back as long as he has an IV in. He has to have that to hydrate him. They won't take it out until we know that his feeding tube is working."

I didn't want to believe her. How many other things did they get wrong? "Where can I make a phone call from my cell phone?" I asked her. "I'm calling the group home."

"You can call from right here," she replied. Normally, you can't make cell phone calls from inside a hospital, but I knew she didn't want me wandering the halls making a fuss.

I dialed the group home. The director, Amy, answered. I asked her, "I'm at the hospital with Ray. He was supposed to be released today, and now they're telling us that the group home won't take him back if he has IVs. Is that true?"

"Yes," she replied

I was deflated. I thanked Amy and hung up. I looked back at the nurse. "I'd like to speak to Dr. Dansk," I said. The nurse left the room without saying another word. I wished that she was a patient in that hospital. Then, maybe she would understand what we've been going through for the past four weeks.

I sat on the edge of Ray's bed again. My brain was mush. I didn't know what to do, how to fight this ineptness. I couldn't fathom this whole nightmare. How could this be happening?

"I'm sorry Ray-Ray. I'm so, so sorry," I said to him. I had tried so hard. I had fought so much, and still it wasn't enough. I was confounded. I was stunned. I was speechless. I just sat on Ray's bed with my head in my hands.

My cell phone rang. It was Ray's advocate, Jean. She said, "I'm so sorry. I've been on vacation. I was listening to my messages, and I just had to call you. What's going on?" It was so good to hear her voice: someone on my side to help me fight for Ray.

I told her, "Jean, I'm at the hospital in Ray's room. He was supposed to be released today. Now they tell me the home won't take him. Every day I wake up thinking that this nightmare will be over, and every day it continues." My voice started cracking. "Do I have a right to be upset?"

"Of course you do." I need to be reassured once in a while because I'm being made to feel like I'm overreacting.

"I just found out that the group home could have made arrangements to have someone be with Ray all this time, and they didn't," I told her.

There was a moment of dead silence; then she said, "I'm going to call the group home and tell them that they have to send someone to be with Ray until he's released. Will that be okay?"

Okay? I wanted to reach through the phone and kiss her. "Thank you!" I told her. That's what Ray needed all along—someone to be with him when his family couldn't.

After that, I was in a quandary. Should I stay with Ray, or should I go home and get some much-needed rest? He looked so pathetic.

He was still in his chair, something I hadn't seen in all the weeks he'd been in the hospital. His eyes kept closing, and he was slumped over. Those stupid mitts had been on his hands for two days, and I doubted if they'd ever been taken off.

My cell phone rang again. Amy from the group home was on the line. She said, "I can't send someone down to be with Ray. I'm short-staffed, and I have another person in the hospital who is a behavioral problem. I have to have someone with him twenty-four hours a day." She sounded like I was asking for something preposterous.

"So, you're telling me that because Ray isn't causing problems, he has to spend another night alone because I can't be with him twenty-four hours a day? I just found out that arrangements could have been made for someone to be with Ray while he's in the hospital," I said to her.

"Who told you that?" she asked.

I gave names, but what difference did it make where I got this information? Was I right or wrong? "Well, that isn't necessarily so," she said.

I said, "Well, I've seen people sitting with him when he was at the hospital near his group home."

"I only had four days' notice," was her reply. What? It takes more than four days to pick up a phone and call Firstcare?

"He's been in the hospital for four weeks," I stated. I found it hard to believe that in four weeks she couldn't have arranged to have someone stay in the hospital for even part of that time.

"I'm having a hard time getting people to come in," she replied. "With the holidays, I'm understaffed."

Working for a government agency, I understand that there are certain policies that have to be followed, but when you're dealing with sick people, you have to have a procedure for situations like Ray's. Besides, my friend's brother was under the NYS DDSO also and was taken care of by someone from Firstcare. That group home didn't have as much notice as Ray's home did. None of Amy's excuses appeased me.

Finally, Amy said, "I can't have someone stay with Ray twenty-four hours a day." The behavioral problem can. Why not Ray? I thought.

"I don't want someone for twenty-four hours a day, just at night, when I can't be here," I told her. Where were the people who were supposed to be looking out for Ray's best interest? "This place is a nightmare," I said. "I can't believe the treatment that Ray's getting. IVs out, in the dark, lying in his own urine…"

"Well, your parents agreed to send Ray there," she said.

Oh, so now the blame was being laid elsewhere. "My parents are not in the medical field. They were going by others' recommendations. So, are you telling me it's my parents' responsibility to make sure Ray is getting proper treatment?" I asked her.

"No," she replied.

"So, if a person from a group home is put in a hospital, is it the group home's responsibility to make sure he gets good treatment?" I asked.

"Well, no it's up to the hospital," she said.

"So, if a person from a group home is in the hospital, the hospital is solely responsible for that person?" I asked.

"Well, no," she replied.

"Why did I have to talk to the patient advocate, the director of nurses, and Ray's advocate to have them put in his chart that he be checked every hour? And they're talking about sending him back to your group home and putting him back in here again to replace his tube," I said.

"Well, I can assure you that he won't be left alone the next time he is sent there," she told me.

I said, "He never should have been left alone in the first place." With that, I hung up.

What a mess this was, and no one wanted to take responsibility. Everyone was spinning around in circles, trying to place the blame elsewhere, and my head was spinning, trying to sort everything out. Oh, I wanted to kick people, and wring their necks, and shout from the rooftops, but they would lock me up, and what good would that do for Ray? I had to calm myself down, or I would have a heart attack. Then I'd be in the cardiac ward of this very hospital.

"Thank you, Pat. Thank you for everything," Mom tried to reassure me.

Thank me for what? "What did I do?" I asked. I had accomplished nothing, absolutely nothing. All of my energy, both physical and mental, was used up, and I had accomplished absolutely nothing. A friend told me once that I was like the Energizer Bunny. I just keep going and going and going. Well, the Energizer Bunny died today in that room.

Dr. Dansk hadn't shown up yet, so I went out to the nurses' station and asked again to speak to her. After all, she was the one who verified that Ray would be released today. She came after only a few minutes of being paged. In her Slavic accent, she said, "I don't know why the group home can't take your brother with an IV. His tube is working properly. He could be released if they would take him."

I don't understand myself. Why is an IV more of a problem than a feeding tube? I don't understand why Jill said that the home agreed to take Ray when there were stipulations on what condition they would take him. I don't know anything anymore. I think everyone involved has messed up and no one wants to admit it.

I wanted to wheel Ray out into the hallway, down the elevators, and into the lobby so that everyone could see how bad he was. Maybe, then, he would get the attention that he deserved. But I couldn't do that. I would have to fight another day. First, we needed to get Ray out of that hospital and back to his group home, where he gets so much care and attention.

Mom and I stayed for about one more hour. I hated to leave Ray in his chair with those stupid mitts on because I didn't know when he'd be put back in bed. His face was cringing as if he was in pain. Mom was getting tired, and I couldn't handle more of her sad stories about other places that Ray had been and the deplorable conditions that he had endured.

As I was leaving Ray's room, I had a flashback to the times I felt pangs of sadness when leaving my father-in-law and sister-in-law lying all alone in their coffins in the funeral home. Again I was leaving a loved one behind, and there wasn't a thing that I could do about it.

December 24, Saturday

I called the group home and spoke to Amy at about 10:45 AM. She said that Don from Ray's group home had been at West End since 9:00 AM. I called the nurses' station on Ray's floor to see what was going on with Ray's release. The person answering said, "We're trying. We need to get a doctor to release him." Don was patiently waiting, with Ray all dressed to leave and ready to go back to the group home.

By 12:00 PM, I still had not received a call from the group home or the hospital. I called the nurses' station again. "I'm checking on the progress of Raymond — — —. Has he been released yet?" I asked.

"He's being released today. We're working on it," I was told.

No kidding. I knew that. Why do they think that I keep calling? Do they think that I have all of the time in the world to waste trying to get answers from their staff? It's less stressful delivering a baby than it is trying to get information from that hospital.

Finally, finally, I got a call from my mom. Ray had been released. I feel like a great weight has been lifted from my shoulders. Ray is out of that hellhole.

"Thank you for taking care of Ray, Pat," Mom said.

"It's not over, Mom. We want to make sure that this doesn't happen to him again. No one should have to endure what Ray has," I told her.

I'm not usually a fighter. My body doesn't handle stress well anymore. I only fight when a terrible indignity is done or when something completely ludicrous happens. Then I fight to the finish, but always, always at the expense of my health.

My heartbeat has been erratic for weeks. I've had a hard time sleeping. My hands are shaking. My mind keeps wandering. My mental state is — well, it's perpetually numb to everything else but Ray. It's been like that since I first saw him in the hospital, 3½ weeks ago.

I could have let everything go very easily once Ray was released from the hospital. I could have washed my hands of the whole fiasco and gone about my life as if nothing happened, but that's not like me. What happened to Ray was so wrong, and there was talk that he would be put in that hospital again. I had to do something so that he wouldn't be treated like he had been ever again, but I didn't know what I needed to do. "Ray-Ray you have to show me a sign," I said to the heavens, as if my message was going to be teleported to Ray. "Ray's angels, you have to show me what to do," I implored. I knew that *they* would hear me.

After I knew that Ray was at his group home being doted on, I could turn my attention to all of my menial tasks. I needed to wash my hair. I couldn't remember the last time I did that, maybe a week before. I knew that I took a bath two days ago because I had a doctor's appointment; but I didn't have enough time to wash my hair then.

I washed and dried my hair, then got ready for Christmas Eve at my sister-in-law, Katherine's, house. After that, I called the group home to see how Ray was. "He's smiling away. He's happy to be home," the aide said.

They put Don on the phone. I told him, "Thanks for getting Ray. That place is like a zoo. Isn't it? I know that you can't say much, but West End is crazy."

"Well, it took a while for the paperwork to get taken care of," he agreed.

What?! It took three hours! All they needed was for a doctor to sign off.

Was it me? Was I getting too upset? Why was everyone making me feel that way? Maybe I'm just too sensitive right now.

I had Monday, the day after Christmas, off. I informed Don, "I was thinking about coming down on Monday to see Ray. Would that be all right?"

"Sure. He usually goes to daycare on that day," he said.

"Do you really think that he's going anywhere on Monday?" I asked. Really, the poor man must have been so weak. I know he lost a lot of weight.

"You're probably right," he replied. "Just call before you come."

I had to see Ray in a better place. The only vision I had of him was the one from the hospital. I had to replace it with a good vision.

Christmas Eve at Katherine's house was very melancholy without Mike's dad and sister. I was too tired to celebrate anything, anyway. After leaving the party at Katherine's house, Mike, Paul, and I went to midnight Mass at our church. I positioned myself directly behind the person in front of me so that Fr. Murphy wouldn't see me with my eyes closed. I really, really wanted to sleep, but for some reason couldn't do it in that church.

December 25, Sunday

I can't believe it's Christmas. Somehow, I had muddled through all of these days, and Christmas was upon me. Thank God for Mike. He sent out all of the holiday cards and went grocery shopping for Christmas dinner. He also stuffed the turkey and cooked it. We're only having twelve family members over for dinner this year, down from over twenty when the whole family shows up.

Early in the day, I called my brothers to wish them a Merry Christmas. The one from Georgia was very cheerful. The other one from Massachusetts had such a bad year that he wasn't celebrating Christmas. He didn't have money to buy Christmas presents.

I tried to make him feel better. "Just remember, Christmas is one day out of the year. And not everyone is celebrating Christmas today. Pretend you belong to some other religion," I suggested. People make way too much of this holiday; then when it doesn't turn out like it's portrayed in the movies, they get so depressed.

Who said that Christmas had to be perfect with lots of presents and lots of people loving each other? Sure, it would be great if people were generous and gave out lots of presents, and everyone was all lovey-dovey and hugged and got along; but that's not how the world is. Why should we expect anything different on Christmas?

I felt badly ending the call to my brother, but I had to get the house ready for Christmas dinner.

Dinner was uneventful. While Mike's sister, Katherine, and I did dishes, we talked about how everyone is having such a hard time dealing with the deaths in the family. I feel badly because I haven't had time to help my loved ones who are hurting so much. Raymond has taken up so much of my time, but he needs me now.

Everyone left by 9:00 PM. Mike and I cleaned up the rest of the dishes and straightened up the house and then went to bed. Merry Christmas to all, and thank God it's good night.

December 26, Monday

I needed to see Ray at his group home just to assure myself that he was okay. I know that he's well taken care of there. I was going to go with Mike to just run in for a quick visit. I gave my mother a courtesy call, so that she didn't think I was doing things behind her back.

She wanted to go, but she was still in her pajamas. "I'm leaving now, but if you can be dressed in twenty minutes I'll pick you up," I told her.

"I can be ready. I'd like to see how Ray is doing," she said. With that, Mike and I picked up my mom and journeyed over to see Ray.

When we got to Ray's group home, he was fully clothed and in his wheelchair. Even with clothes on, you could tell that he lost a lot of weight. He looked so tired. Even so, he beamed when he saw us. I sat on a chair by Ray and held his hand. He looked too tired to do anything else.

I saw that there were two other residents with feeding tubes that looked like Ray's. I wondered if any of the other residents in Ray's home had ever had trouble with their feeding tubes, and, if so, what happened to them. I was afraid to ask. My mother didn't want me to question the people at the group home because they were nice and were taking good care of Raymond. I was just wanted to get answers.

After about an hour, the residents were gently led or placed in wheelchairs one by one to be taken to their rooms for an afternoon nap. Finally, Ray was ready to go back to bed, too. I wished that I could take a nap with him. I felt as exhausted as he looked.

As we were leaving, my mom was talking to one of the workers at the group home about how hard it is to get answers from West End Community Hospital. I jumped into the conversation with, "That's why the patient advocate said that you and Dad should sign something allowing me or Lynn to have information on Ray, too."

I looked at the aide with whom we were talking. "Do you know how that's done?" I asked.

"No. You should probably talk to Amy. She's the director. She should know. She'll be in tomorrow. You can talk to her then," I was told.

After we left the group home, we headed to Molly's Eatery less than a mile down the road for some down home cooking. Oh, their food was so good. I shoved food in my face until I felt like my stomach was going to explode. Comfort food is a wonderful thing.

December 27, Tuesday

I called Mom from work today. "Good morning. I just called to remind you to call Amy at the group home," I said.

"Why?" she asked.

"What do you mean, why, Mom?" I said. "Don't you remember when we were at the group home yesterday, they said that Amy would be in today? Aren't you going to call her to ask how I can get information on Raymond?"

"Oh, I forgot," she said.

How could she forget something like that? Was I being too obsessive? I just wanted things in place for when Ray has to go back into the hospital. It's not a matter of if he goes — it's a matter of when he goes. I want to be able to talk more easily with Ray's nurses and doctors when that happens.

December 28, Wednesday

My mother called me at work this morning. "I tried calling you all morning. Your voice mail said you weren't in," she admonished me.

My voice mail never says I'm out. It always says I'm not available, but will return the call as soon as possible. "I was here. I may have been on the phone, but I've been here all day," I told her.

"Well," she said, "I called Amy, and she said that I needed to speak with Joe Griffin [Raymond's Medicaid case manager]. I called him, and he said that he's never heard of giving a sister permission to have information on a consumer [what wards of the NYS DDSO are called], just the parents, but he'll look into it."

"Okay," I replied.

"Pat, you have to stop fighting so much. Ray is in his group home, now," she said. Does she want me to forget everything that happened to Ray?

"Ray never should have gotten the treatment he did. And I want to see that it never happens again, Mom," I told her.

After I hung up the phone, I sat at my desk, stunned. I'm sure that she said what she did to try to calm me down, but it did the opposite to me. The emotions I had felt these past weeks came to the surface all at once, and I couldn't stop crying.

I know what I'm doing is right, but sometimes I need assurance from someone else. I had to go over to my friend, Ginny's, workstation for consolation. She's been my own personal pep squad. Whenever I need an ego boost, she gives it to me. "You're Ray's guardian angel. You're his hope," she told me. That's what I needed to hear. I stopped blubbering and sat down at my desk to work.

When I can't concentrate at work, I write. I keep writing and writing. My list of names of people I've spoken to, and what they've said, and what condition I've found Ray in gets longer and longer. My journal is growing. I don't know what I'm going to do with it, but I feel compelled to write. I have to tell Ray's story. I don't know who I'll tell it to or how to tell it, but I'm confident that God will show me at the right time.

January 12–16, 2006

For five blissful days, I forgot about the world and my past tribulations. A trip to Florida was just what I needed. The sun was wonderful. The warmer weather was soothing. Occasionally, I was compelled to talk about poor Ray. Mike, Paul, and I were visiting family. How could I not talk about Ray if they asked about him?

I drank. I played cards. I laughed. I smoked cigars. I sang. I drove around in a convertible with the top down in seventy-degree weather. Sure, it was a bit cold, but I just put my jacket hood up over my head and let the wind whip around my face. Almost anything could have been better than what my brother and my family had just endured back home. Paul kept looking at me and Mike and shaking his head in disbelief. Hey, we had been in hell and now we were in paradise. Anyone who had gone through that would be acting a bit ditzy.

On January 16 Paul and I had to head back home. Mike and his mom were staying in Florida for a while longer. I didn't want to go home to what awaited me, but I won't run from my life. The way I deal with things is to go at them head on and face them. I'd hate myself if I ran away.

For a few short hours on the plane, I was in a peaceful limbo. I was nowhere and didn't have to deal with anything. It was just me in my seat with my books and my journal. Maybe when I go home, I can lead a normal life once more. I prayed for normalcy again.

January 17, Tuesday

I woke up late—7:15 AM. Darn! I wasn't going to make it to work on time. I got ready, and waited until 8:00 AM to call in late, and left for work. Not bad. I made it in by 8:30, only a half hour late.

I couldn't get my phone to change my voice mail message to say that I was in. It took me another half hour to get that working. The rest of my work day was just as chaotic.

I had to rush home after work and go grocery shopping. The grocery store had a buy-one-get-one-free chicken Caesar salad. Perfect—one for my dinner tonight and one for my lunch tomorrow, if Paul didn't eat it before then. Speaking of Paul, he had had a 3:30 PM class and still wasn't home by 6:45 PM. I was getting concerned. I called his phone, but got a recording to dial a ten-digit voice mailbox. I had no idea what that number was.

Lynn called to welcome me home, but I had to cut her off because I had to be at a meeting for the decorating committee for an event at the Knights of Columbus in five minutes. Once I got there, my brother called me to see if I had made it home uneventfully. I had to cut him off, too, because the meeting was starting. Great, people never call me when I'm home; now I go out of town and have all kinds of people calling me to welcome me back.

The meeting ended early, and I went home to finish unpacking. I called Lynn back. We talked about trivial things. Then the bomb fell. "Did you talk to Mom?" she asked.

I hadn't called her. I knew that she didn't remember when I was leaving, so I figured that she wouldn't know when I was getting back, either. Anyway, I knew Lynn asking me wasn't a good thing.

"Well, she was afraid to call you," she said. Oh God, now what? I knew it had to do with Ray.

"Ray was taken to West End to have his tube taken out," she told me.

"Not again?" I exclaimed. "That's, what, the fourth one, isn't it? What are they doing? Why can't they just get it right? Why do they have to keep putting Ray through this?"

"Well, he's been in since Thursday. He's only supposed to be in there a week. What a difference. His care is so much better. They had him on a different floor, and he seemed to be getting more attention," she said.

"Well, they knew that they had to. I discussed that with Ray's case manager, Joe Griffin. When Ray went back, Joe was going to see what steps could be taken for Ray to get better care," I told Lynn.

Why does everyone have to be categorized? Ray has an adult body, so he's put in a ward that treats only adults. But he has the mind of a child. Why can't someone with the mentality of a child be in a ward with children? Then Ray might get the attention he deserves. At least the surroundings would be more cheerful.

"They put an IV in Ray's arm and took out the tube in his stomach so that his stomach can heal. Then they're going to put Ray into a nursing home for about a month while his stomach heals, and then they are going to put a tube back into his stomach. He's going to Northbrook Nursing Home," Lynn said.

"Northbrook? Why there?" I asked. "That's not in a good area. That can't be the only place they can send him."

"I know. I heard they have to lock you in there," she said.

"Lynn, why are they putting him *there*?" I asked.

"Mom kept saying, 'Oh, if Pat were here, she would be so mad,'" Lynn said.

"Well, yeah. I can't figure it out, Lynn," I said. "Why can't they get Ray's feeding tube to work? There are a lot of people with feeding tubes that are working. Why can't they get Ray's to work? That's all. That's all I want to know. And no one I talk to can tell me."

"I don't know, Pat," Lynn said. "Something else happened while you were gone. Mom fell down and hurt her knee really badly."

"Not again," I said. "Why are Mom and Dad always falling?"

"I don't know. Dad's been good with Ray. Poor Dad went down to see Ray by himself yesterday, and I guess he had to turn back because he was in so much pain. He thinks he has some cracked ribs," she told me. "He came back home and put a support thing on like you had when you pulled the muscles in your side," Lynn said.

"Yeah, you have to be careful with those things," I said, "especially when you have cracked ribs. If it's too tight, it can cause your broken ribs to puncture a lung."

"Well, I went to see Ray today. He wasn't smiling much, but he didn't seem as agitated this time in the hospital," she said.

"He's still on pain medication isn't he?" I asked. "I wouldn't be complaining if I was on pain meds either."

"Well, I just wanted to tell you about Ray," she finished.

"Thanks," I said. And we hung up.

Will there ever be an end to poor Ray's torture? How many tubes are they going to put in and take out? They're starving the poor man.

While I was getting ready for bed I talked to my reflection in the mirror. I've been talking to myself a lot lately. Is that normal? Anyway, I said to my reflection, "Remember when you prayed for normalcy? Not gonna happen. Welcome home."

January 18, Wednesday

Mom called me at home after work. I let her tell me everything about Ray. Then she told me how she hurt her knee.

"I know, Mom, Lynn told me. She said you were afraid to call me. Why, Mom?" I asked. "I don't yell at you."

"Well, you lecture me," she replied.

"Oh," I said, "now I'm the bad guy again." Why do we always seem to be at odds?

"Amy at the group home told me that Ray was so bad the second time they took him to the hospital, that they didn't even know if he would make it through the ride to West End," Mom went on.

"Well, why did they let him get so bad?" I wanted to know.

"She said that they never should have let him leave the hospital. He wasn't getting any nutrition through the last feeding tube," she told me.

"The doctor told us they had to test the feeding tube before they sent him back to his group home. That's why he wasn't released on the day that they said he would be. It must have been working," I said.

"Amy said that we complained about the treatment of Ray at the hospital and didn't want him to be sent back there," she said.

"Well, we did complain, Mom," I said. "We didn't want him to be sent back there. Yet, he's there, isn't he? And they let him almost die before they sent him back." They're trying to blame us again for his deplorable treatment. We're not doctors or nurses! Why are they blaming us for his condition?

I can't talk to Mom anymore without getting upset. Part of the reason is that Dad is a man of few words. He doesn't like talking on the phone, making Mom always the bearer of the frustrating news about Ray. She's confounded and exhausted by all that is happening, and I'm getting perturbed trying to get information from her.

I once read a book about emotions, and it said that underneath anger is a deep, deep hurt. The author is right. I hurt. I hurt. I really hurt. It hurts me to see Ray. It hurts to talk to my mom. It hurts to feel so helpless. It hurts to be blamed for things that I didn't do. Every day I hurt.

I know that I'm doing the right thing, though. I'm going to keep asking questions and getting on people's backs if Ray isn't treated right. I can't turn my back on Ray and walk away.

January 19, Thursday

I went with Lynn to see Raymond. This was my first visit with him since he was back in the hospital on a different floor. It's hard to imagine, but he's lost even more weight. He reminded me of those pictures of the Holocaust victims when the troops first freed them from the concentration camps. They were walking carcasses. Well, Ray looked like a carcass in a fetal position with two holes in his stomach.

While we were in Ray's room, his former roommate came in to see how he was doing. Lynn filled me in on who he was. For the first few days that Ray was on the floor, this dear, sweet man was Ray's roommate. He had open-heart surgery. When Ray would cry in the middle of the night, this man would go over and comfort him. Now, even though he was given a new room, he still checked on Ray. Today he brought some balloons. "I don't need all of these," he said. "I thought that I'd bring some over for Ray."

Soon a nurse came in. I could see by the way Ray's face lit up when she walked into the room that she was taking extra special care of him. The nurse said to me and Lynn, "On the days that I work, I ask to take care of Ray." She was Ray's guardian angel as long as he was on that floor. How could two floors in the same hospital be as different as night and day?

"I was thinking of maybe putting Ray in his wheelchair today, but I'm not quite sure how to do it. Have you ever put Ray in his chair?" that cherub of a nurse asked me and Lynn.

Lynn and I looked at each other, dumbfounded. "At the group home and on the other floor in this hospital, they used a lift to get him in his chair," I offered.

"Well, I've never used one, but let me go get one, and maybe we can figure out how to do it," she said. Wow, a nurse who's willing to go the extra mile for Ray. On the other floor, the nurses I saw either didn't care or didn't have the time to do anything except what was absolutely necessary, and at times they didn't even do that.

Not much time passed before Ray's nurse came back into the room, pushing a contraption on wheels with a big arm that had a hook on the end to which a cloth chair-like apparatus was attached. The nurse pushed a button that lowered the hook down. She took the chair-like thing down and laid it on the bed beside Ray's back.

She said, "Now, I think that if we kind of roll Ray on his side, we can slide this around his body and position the bottom on Ray's butt. Then we'll raise him up, and swing him into his chair. You ladies just stay on the sides of him. Then get his wheelchair and put it under him as soon as he's far enough away from the bed." It seemed complicated. The people in the group home made it look so easy.

We figured it out eventually, and Ray was in his wheelchair without mishap. He was slumped over more than he should have been, but hey, we didn't drop him or hurt him. Ray had a look on his face as if he wasn't sure if he should be happy or crying.

"Okay girls," the nurse said. "Why don't you take Ray for a walk around the floor? One of you take Ray's IV pole, and one take the chair." Lynn and I smiled at each other. We knew Ray would love that. He loves being around people.

We were soon walking Ray around the floor. "Look at you, Ray," or "Hi, Ray," the workers said as they saw us wheeling him down the hallway. The workers on *this* floor sure knew who he was. They all waved as we were taking our stroll.

Ray looked—well he looked crabby. We rolled down the hall until we found Ray's ex-roommate's room. He looked surprised. "Hey, Ray. Now you're coming to visit me," he said.

We tried to roll Ray's chair into the room, but the room was too small. The other man in the room gave us a look like, why are you bringing this creature into my room? Lynn and I didn't want that man to get all stressed out, so we quickly backed out of the room and walked down the rest of the long hallway. Back to Ray's room we went, down at the very end of the floor. I think he was put there because he makes a lot of noise when he's upset.

It was time for Lynn and me to leave, but we didn't want to just abandon Ray in the chair in his room all by himself. We found his nurse and told her that we were leaving. "Bring Ray down to the nurses' station when you leave. That way he'll be around people," she told us. What a sweetie she was.

We parked Ray in his wheelchair by the nurses' desk. He beamed from ear to ear as we left, like he had just found his harem. He loved the ladies.

The group home didn't arrange for someone to be with Ray when he was admitted to the hospital again, like I was promised by the director. It was too late for me to complain now. He was supposed to be released to Northbrook in a few days. At least he was getting better care on this floor.

January 20, Friday

I'm alternating between sweating profusely and shivering. My body is so confused. I don't know if I'm coming down with a cold or if it's just stress.

I called Raymond's Medicaid case manager, Joe Griffin, early this morning.

"Hi, Joe," I said. "I was just wondering if West End Community Hospital said that Ray would be released only to Northbrook because his doctor practices there."

Joe didn't seem to think so. I explained to him that my dad is hard-of-hearing, has three cracked ribs, and that my mom fell down and hurt her knee. "They're both going to be 80 years old this year. This whole thing has just worn them out. And trying to get information from the hospital is like beating your head against a wall," I explained.

"Jean Jeffors e-mails me every few days," Joe told me. "She should e-mail me on Ray's progress. I'll call you after I check some things and tell you if I have information from Jean."

I've found a friend in Joe. I need someone who is willing to talk to me and get answers to my questions. I think he's being unrealistic that Ray will go back to his group home, but I have to give him credit for remaining hopeful in the midst of all of this crap.

I hung up the phone, and it just hit me: Wow, my parents are going to be 80 years old this year. When did they get that old? No wonder why they're exhausted by everything that's going on. Was I being too hard on my aging parents?

I called my parents' house and, of course, talked to my mom. "Mom," I asked, "did you ask the person who releases people from the hospital if Northbrook was the only place where Ray could go?"

"Why?" she wanted to know.

"Northbrook isn't really in a great section of town," I replied. "I haven't heard anything good about that place. Is that the only place where he can go?"

"I don't know," she said. "Why? It probably is."

"Mom, don't you want to know for sure? Do you really trust that hospital to give you the correct information without verifying it?" I asked.

"Well, how would I get that information?" she asked.

"Just ask the person who works on releasing the hospital patients. You know, like that Jill person who said Ray was going to be released? The one who wasn't there on the day that she said Ray was going home," I explained.

"Well, if they said Northbrook, then they have to send him there," she said.

"Mom, I find it hard to believe that Northbrook is the only place in a big city that can take care of him. There must be another choice. Is that the only place he can go? If it is, don't you want to know why?" I asked.

"Pat, what do you want me to do?" she said, all defensive. Doesn't she want to know if Ray has more options?

"You know what Mom, I want to help Ray; but I feel like you don't want me to. So, you know what? I'm not going to. I'm not going to do anything for Ray anymore. I'm not going to talk to you about him anymore."

I hung up on her. I hung up on my mother. Darn! I was just questioning whether I was being too hard on my parents, and there I was, hanging up on my mom. I'm usually a better person than this. This whole ordeal is screwing up my emotions and fraying my nerves. I feel so much anger and pain, and I don't know what to do about it.

My dear friend, Donna, called me at work to see how I was and to offer to drop me off and pick me up if I wanted to see Ray. I thanked Donna and told her that I may take her up on her offer someday. Sometimes you don't realize what wonderful friends you have until you're going through hard times. I am truly blessed with many good friends.

I got Paul to go to the hospital with me today. I just wanted someone to walk with me from the parking garage to the hospital in the dark. He's a tall, husky young man, and I don't think anyone would mess with him. He also has a black belt in karate, although I don't know if he would use it in self-defense.

I didn't want to make Paul come up to Ray's room with me. He's been through enough grief in these past few months with the passing away of his grandfather and his aunt. I wouldn't feel right if I dumped more grief on him. Paul had never seen Ray, and I thought that it would be a shock for him to see Ray for the first time in the condition he was in—a gray-haired man all bent up and crippled, crying, and emitting unintelligible noises.

I, on the other hand, hardly notice Ray's ailments anymore. When I look at him, all I see is a gentle creature, all alone in a hospital, who needs comforting.

Paul plopped himself in the comfy, overstuffed chairs in the lobby and read his school book while I, once more, went up the elevator, then walked down the long, lonely hall to Ray's room.

Ray wasn't smiling like yesterday. Today he was so pathetic looking. He kept growling like he does when he's upset. He was lying on his side and constantly rubbing his head. His whole body was burning as if he had a fever. I couldn't stay for long because I had promised Paul that I wouldn't. I just needed to see Ray. The way he looked made me wonder if he would make it out of West End to be released to a nursing home. I left his room, crying again. I wonder how my body can produce tears continually for two months and not become dehydrated.

I dropped Paul off at home and drove to the airport to pick up Mike. While I sat waiting for his plane to land, I had time to think. I have so much hurt inside of me. It feels as if someone is stabbing me in the heart. I keep writing and writing because that's how I get to the bottom of my feelings. I ran out of paper to write on, so I picked up some flyers that were on the airport seats and wrote in their margins.

I realized that I feel as if no one appreciates my fighting for Ray. That hurts. It isn't easy for me. This whole mess is physically taking a toll on me. I'm getting chest pains, and it scares me.

As much as that upset me, that wasn't where my deepest pain came from. It came from thinking of Ray alone and misunderstood. I feel part of the reason that the hospital staff is ignoring Ray is because they can't communicate with him. All his ailments make him that much more unpleasant to be around. I see the look in some of the staff's eyes. Raymond is not a cute little boy or a handsome man. To them he's a freak.

I know what it's like to be ignored, to not be wanted. When I was young, I was painfully shy. My tongue would freeze. My mouth would dry up. Words would get stuck in my throat, and my hands would shake when I was in the midst of people. Boys didn't want to date someone who wore glasses and stumbled over her words. I'd be the last one picked by team captains in gym because my nervousness made me so uncoordinated. I felt like a freak. I know what it's like to not be wanted, to not be able to communicate. That's why when I'm with Ray I feel we're two kindred spirits—two lonely, misunderstood souls.

I couldn't live with myself if I stopped fighting for Ray. And I just have to accept the fact that my mom's not the fighter that she used to be. She just isn't going to fight as much as I am, right now. I can't follow through with what I said about not doing anything for Ray. What I need to do is what feels right for me, and that is to do whatever I can to help Ray.

I did mean what I said about not talking to my mother about Raymond. My mother was right. I do have to stop fighting so much. I have to stop fighting with her. We both can't handle that aggravation right now.

Mike's plane was late. I just wanted to go home to bed and lay my head on my wonderfully soft pillow. The days are so long when you go through them with a heavy heart. I tried to remember what life was like before October of last year. I wondered if my life would ever be without sorrow or pain again.

As I sat watching the people at the airport, I saw loved ones hugging each other as they were reunited. Everyone should be so loved. Everyone should have someone waiting anxiously for their return. Finally, I was the one giving my loved one a hug as he got off of the plane.

My day wasn't over when I got home. I had to call Lynn for an update on Ray. She informed me that Ray has yet another doctor. This is the second one in a week. Dr. Schneider is the new one's name. He's under the teaching part of the hospital, which makes me wonder if Ray is being used as a guinea pig. I'm always assured that the hospital has a top-notch staff. They're only top-notch if you can get them to take care of Ray properly.

Finally, it was bedtime for me. The circles under my eyes get darker and darker by the day. I don't remember waking up at night, yet when I get up in the morning, I'm exhausted like I didn't sleep. I'm sure it has something to do with the slow boiling anger that I'm harboring. I just can't believe what is being allowed to happen to

Ray, even though I'm bringing it to the attention of everyone that I can.

I'd complain to Ray's doctor, but they are constantly changing, just as his nurses seem to change. No one at that hospital takes care of Ray long enough to get to know him. If they did, I'm sure they'd take better care of him. How could you not want to take good care of such a helpless, gentle creature? At least he's getting better care now that he's on a different floor.

January 21, Saturday

I called the nurses' station on Ray's floor and asked to speak to Ray's doctor. The woman who answered said that she had to look for the phone number. A few minutes later, a man with a Hindu accent got on the phone and identified himself as a doctor. I couldn't understand his name, let alone what he was saying. There was no way I was going to ask him questions about Ray's condition. I have a hard time understanding what's happening to him when I hear it in English. I'm certainly not going to try understanding Ray's predicament from someone with a Hindu accent.

"I was hoping that I could speak to Dr. Schneider," I said.

"I can give him a message," the doctor replied.

"He'll call me back today?" I inquired. I was impressed because it was a Saturday and no doctor ever called me on a Saturday unless there was an emergency.

"Yes," he replied. I gave the Hindu doctor my cell phone number and put the cell phone in my jeans pocket. I went about my business, patiently waiting for the doctor to call.

At one point during the day, I had to go to the bathroom. I flushed the toilet, pulled up my slacks, and then heard a loud, resounding, "Plunk!" I looked into the toilet and saw my cell phone. With lightning speed that I didn't know I possessed, I reached down and retrieved my phone out of the toilet bowl. It had only been in the water for seconds. How much damage could be done?

I looked at the phone. Darn! It had turned off, and I couldn't turn it back on. Darn! I took the phone to Mike, hoping somehow that he could perform a miracle and get it working. But I wasn't going to be blessed with a miracle today. My phone wasn't going to work. Now, how was I going to get a phone call from Ray's doctor?

I called the nurses' station on Raymond's floor again and asked to speak to Dr. Schneider. The nurse who answered said, "A doctor who? What floor does he work on?"

"He's treating my brother Raymond, who's on your floor," I told her.

"Oh, I see," she said. "He's part of the blah-blah clinic." I didn't get the name of the clinic, but she gave me a phone number to call.

The clinic was closed. No big surprise. It was a Saturday. The recording at the clinic had another phone number to call. I called the phone number the recording gave me and got an answering service. I told the woman at the answering service, "I left a message with Dr. Schneider to call me about my brother, who's a patient of West End Hospital. I gave him my cell phone number, but I dropped my phone in the toilet." That got a chuckle from the woman on the other end. "I'd like to leave another phone number where he can contact me." She took down the message.

After that, I went to Lynn's house for Jenny's party. Mom and Dad didn't come. Mom couldn't walk because her knee was still hurting. I offered to carry her into Lynn's house, but she declined.

All I could think of all day long was how I wanted to go to bed early. I came home about 9:00 PM. I got my wish about 9:30 PM.

Dr. Schneider never called me back. All of my efforts had been for naught.

January 22, Sunday

I just realized that I've been much calmer since I haven't talked to Mom about Ray. Oh, I talk to her, but if there's anything about Ray that I have to discuss, I ask to speak with Dad. I'm sure my mom is calmer too without me fighting with her.

Lynn and I went together to see Ray again. The hospital is waiting for a bed to open before they can release him. I was checking dates in my pocket calendar when a handsome, young Dr. Schneider entered the room, unannounced, with what looked like another resident doctor of Hindu descent.

I stood up quickly, and my calendar with all of my little slips of paper spilled out onto the floor. I felt so scatterbrained. I hoped that Dr. Schneider didn't think likewise. "Dr. Schneider, did you call me yesterday?" I asked him. "Because my cell phone fell in the toilet." Now he'll think I'm a ditz, I thought to myself.

"Well, I have to admit, no," he answered.

"Well, you could have lied. I wouldn't have known," I joked with him.

He flashed me a brilliant smile, then put his hand up and made a space a couple of inches wide between his thumb and index finger. "I came this close to it," he said.

He could have lied, but he didn't; now I knew that he wouldn't give me a line of bull.

We got down to business. "Do you have any questions?" asked Dr. Schneider. He looked at me, then at Lynn.

"Ray had a fever. Does he still have one?" I asked.

"No, we found antibiotics that have done the trick. We're going to fill out the paperwork for Ray to be transferred to Northbrook," he told us.

Dr. Schneider explained that Raymond's feeding tube was taken out because they couldn't get it to function properly. An IV line called a PICC line was put in. It goes about a foot into a vein in the arm. These are put in when an IV is needed on a more permanent basis. It would take about two months for his stomach to heal, then Ray would come back to the hospital to have a new feeding tube inserted. I couldn't see how two holes in your stomach that have been there for years could heal, but the doctor sounded so positive that I didn't question him.

My dad had told me that doctors couldn't guarantee that the new feeding tube would work. I needed to hear that for myself.

"Is there a guarantee that this new feeding tube will work?" I asked.

Dr. Schneider shook his head in the negative. He waited for that information to sink in. Then he asked again, "Do you have any more questions?" Lynn and I looked at each other, then at the doctor, and shook our heads "no."

"He is lucky to have you," the doctor told us. "And I just want you to know that we gave him the best care that we could."

"Well, we had problems on the other floor he was on, but he seems to be getting better care now," I said. I left it at that. I didn't want to get into how I felt Ray was neglected.

Dr. Schneider finished with, "Okay, if you have no more questions...".

Something nagged at me. What was he waiting for us to ask? Why did he say Ray was lucky to have us? I didn't have time to ponder because Dr. Schneider left the room immediately after that, and then Lynn and I gave Ray our attention.

I went home assured that Ray wasn't being left in deplorable conditions, like on the other floor, and that he was getting the best care possible.

January 27, Friday

Ray was finally released to Northbrook Nursing Home last night.

I've been reminded by the personnel department at my job that I haven't used up all of the personal time coming to me. Perfect. I could divide up that time and leave work early a couple of days so that I could do all of my tasks and take a few naps to stave off my constant exhaustion.

The event at the Knights of Columbus that I volunteered to do decorations for is today. I was planning to leave work early to go see Ray, then go home to take a nap, before heading to the Knights to help with the event.

I parked on the street in front of Northbrook, walked up the long, semicircular drive, and entered the glass-enclosed entrance for the first time. There were no locked doors that my sister, Lynn, said she heard about. Inside, the lobby was spacious. On one side, a wide-screen TV was blaring away, surrounded by residents engrossed in some afternoon talk show.

I went up to the security desk, signed in, and was given a visitor's pass by the helpful guard, who then directed me to the two elevators that led to the other floors. On the third floor, I got off of the elevators and turned right. My dad had given me directions to Ray's room this morning. Through the doors I walked, then stopped at the nurses' station.

"Hi, I'm Raymond — — —'s sister," I said. I was introduced to Ray's doctor, a lovely Hindu woman. Even with her accent, I could understand Dr. Patel perfectly.

"Hello. Your parents were in this morning. I hadn't examined Ray when I saw them, but now I have. His hemoglobin is down from last night," she told me.

I knew that hemoglobin was in the red blood cells, but nothing else. I plied the doctor for more information. "Does that mean he's bleeding internally?" I asked.

"Well, I don't know. He did have a bowel movement, but it wasn't tarry," she said. That's a sign of internal bleeding from the digestive system. "Your family has to decide what you want done with your brother."

"What do you mean?" I asked.

"Well, to see if he's bleeding, we'll have to put a scope down him, but we have to remove him from here, and if he's to have a blood transfusion, he'll have to be removed from here also," she explained.

"Do I have to decide that today?" I asked her. I didn't understand why she was bombarding me with these questions as soon as she saw me. What was the hurry?

"Have you ever thought of comfort care?" she asked.

"What do you mean?" I said. I knew what she was getting at, but my mind didn't want to accept it.

"Well, taking him off of everything and letting him go," she said.

Why was she doing this to me when I was all by myself? I started crying.

"Come on, we'll talk about this someplace else," she said. She whisked me off to the TV and dining room across the hall. We sat at a small, round table. Another woman appeared and introduced herself, but I didn't catch her name.

That woman plopped a box of tissues in front of me. "Can I get you some coffee?" she asked me. I don't normally drink caffeine in the afternoon, but I needed comfort food, so I nodded my head up and down.

The doctor persisted. "The skin on Ray's stomach is breaking down. He's losing protein from the leakage in his stomach," she explained.

As if I didn't know the hole in Ray's stomach was a problem. I had seen it since November. "He's not going to improve," she continued. "The artificial nutrition he's getting isn't supposed to be used to keep someone alive indefinitely. It isn't absorbed by the body the same way as the liquid nutrition that goes into the abdomen."

"But the hospital said that his stomach was going to heal, and that they would put a feeding tube back in," I protested.

"Look at Ray. Do you really think he's going to survive another surgery?" she asked.

It took awhile for that to set in. I resigned myself to the fact that Raymond was going to die.

I recalled the famous family battle in the media over pulling the plug on Terry Schiavo. Her parents were against taking her off of artificial nutrition and hydration. They said that she would suffer from hunger and thirst.

"Will Ray suffer?" I asked.

"No," she replied. "Look at him. He hasn't eaten solid food in years. He hasn't had proper nutrition for months. His weight is down to 70 pounds. He won't suffer any more than he already has. There won't be any pain. We'll make sure that he is comfortable with medication."

I needed time to assimilate all of this information. I just sat and stared at the table. The doctor persisted. "Do you want me to talk to your parents?" she asked. "If you feel uncomfortable, I can speak to them. We can set up an appointment and I can bring it up."

I couldn't have my parents come in and have the doctor pounce on my parents about Ray's plight like she did with me. "No, I'll try to talk to them this weekend. I don't know how they'll feel about this. They're devout Catholics," I explained.

"Oh, I'm not Catholic," the doctor said.

"We have a chaplain who's Catholic, and he's okay with it," the other woman at the table said.

Assured that my family would be thinking about our discussion, the doctor left.

The other woman didn't leave. She introduced herself as the social worker assigned to Ray's floor. There was plenty of paperwork to fill out. A lot of the information asked for I didn't know. "Can I take this to my parents, and get them to fill it out, and bring it in on Monday?" I asked.

"Of course you can, sweetie," she told me. She patted my arm in reassurance. I really wanted to fall into her arms, bawling, and have her comfort me, but I had to be strong or I wasn't going to get through this day.

The social worker couldn't have been nicer or more supportive. She told me how she had lost some of her relatives about as close together in time as I had. Then she divulged to me that she loves to take care of handicapped people because their love is unconditional. No strings attached. They just love everyone. That was Ray. He loved everyone, too.

When we were done, I went down to Ray's room. He lay there, blissfully sleeping away, unaware of the turmoil going on in my heart. I pleaded with him, "Ray-Ray, you have to show me a sign."

He woke up and smiled, then went back to sleep. I sat, then paced, then sat, then paced some more. I cried and prayed that God would help me to make this decision. When I was getting ready to leave the room, I flipped open the folder that held the paperwork the social worker gave me. On the list of phone numbers for contacting the staff at Northbrook was the social worker's name, Emily Archangel. That was my sign. God would be with me all the way. I had an archangel helping me.

I called my friend, Donna, and told her that I wouldn't be able to help her with the event at the Knights of Columbus because I had to speak to my parents about taking Ray off of his IVs. I then went home and prepared myself. In my mind, I knew that I couldn't prolong Ray's suffering. He had lived way too long through artificial means, and it was time for him to go to heaven, where he could be free of pain and be happy.

I went to my parents' house, had dinner, and waited for the opportunity to talk to them about making a decision. "Do you want me to fill out this paperwork, or do you want to?" I asked them.

My mother doesn't want to do anything anymore. She is exhausted by this whole ordeal. My poor dad's hands shake too much to write legibly. So, I filled out sheet after sheet of mindless information, like do we give permission for Northbrook to take pictures, what to do about Ray's laundry, how to get his possessions labeled, and, finally, persons to contact.

I told them, "The doctor wants to know what we want to do about Ray's care. She said that he wasn't going to get better. She asked me if we ever considered comfort care." I explained what it was.

My mother was surprisingly calm about it. She just shook her head. "I knew that this day would come," she said. "You know, doctors asked me to do this before, to let Ray go because he was so bad. Then they never discussed it with me again and he got better." Mom's been through this before. That's why she's not as emotional about this as I am, I thought. She must have done all her crying years ago.

It was about 8:30 PM when I left my parents' house. I went home, put on my fancy clothes, and went to the Knights of Columbus to enjoy the rest of the evening's entertainment. Actually, I was going there to get the love and support that I needed so badly.

As soon as I got there, I was being smothered by hugs and offered alcoholic beverages, which I had to decline because they made my erratic heartbeat worse. I went down to the smoking lounge (the laundry room in the basement of the building) to talk to my closest friends. While I was down there, one of my other friends came down for a smoke. She gave me a hug. "You poor thing, you've been through so much," she comforted me. I knew she hadn't heard about Raymond yet.

"It's not over," I told her. "My family has to decide if we want to take my brother off of the artificial nutrition he's on and let him pass away." Then tears trickled down my face.

With a shocked look on her face, she apologized. "Oh, no. Oh, no. I'm sorry. I made you cry," she said. She kept patting me on the arm. "I'm so, so sorry."

"That's okay," I said. "I've been crying all day. This is a good thing. My brother is suffering so much. We just want it to end. He'll be so much happier in heaven."

Amongst the dirty table linens and smoke-filled air, I tried comforting my usually peppy little friend. I felt badly because she felt so badly about making me feel badly, but I couldn't stop crying. She left without having a cigarette.

The entertainment ended about 10:00 PM, and I helped clean up.

I was in bed by 11:00 PM. What a trying day this has been. My brain is mush and my body is numb.

January 29, Sunday

After Mass at my parish, I asked Fr. Murphy if I could talk to him about my brother. I could see the wheels turning in his head trying to think of a time he could fit me into his busy schedule. "How about 4:00?" he asked.

I've never had a private conversation with a priest about something tugging at my moral conscience. I had always been able to come to terms with it myself, but this, this hastening of my brother's death, was different. I wanted to know what the Catholic church thought about it and why. I needed to know if I would be thought a murderer in the eyes of the church.

Mike and I sat with Fr. Murphy in the kitchen and dining area of the rectory of my parish. I didn't mess around. I got right to the point about how bad my brother was and the decision that I was being asked to make.

"Your brother is being kept alive by artificial means. The church believes that you should not withhold treatment through *natural* means. Like taking food or water away if that person could still swallow, just to end their life," he answered.

"So, you're saying that the church thinks that it's okay to withdraw artificial life-sustaining treatment if it's just prolonging suffering and that person would have died on his own if he didn't have it?" I asked. "The church doesn't believe that a person should be kept alive by any and all means?"

"No, that's a misconception. Your brother is suffering. There is no reason to continue it if he's not going to improve," he said.

"I'm so glad that I talked to you. You made me feel so much better about making this decision," I told him.

Fr. Murphy looked at me and Mike and said, "You two have been through so much."

That was it. He offered no other words of consolation. What words can anyone come up with to make our way more bearable? It would be hard even for those trained in counseling people who are suffering as much as we were. Just acknowledging our pain and looking upon us with his compassionate eyes was enough for me at the time.

I would not be considered a murderer if I made the decision to withdraw Raymond from the artificial liquid that was only prolonging his suffering. There was one less moral issue for me to grapple with. I went to bed with a peaceful mind.

January 30, Monday

This past weekend was spent talking to my brothers and sisters about Ray. I knew in my mind that letting him go was the best thing to do, but I had seen his suffering and his deterioration. My brothers and sister, who lived out of town, hadn't. They needed time to assimilate what had happened to Ray and to examine their hearts to see how they felt about making a decision to pull the plug on their own brother.

By Sunday night, the whole family agreed that we needed to let Ray go. He had suffered enough, both physically and mentally. I couldn't even fathom what must be going through his childlike mind. The poor thing had to suffer alone for hours at a time in a strange place. I had to wipe his picture from my mind, or I wouldn't survive this ordeal with my mental state intact.

This afternoon, my father, mother, Lynn, and I were going to meet with the staff of Northbrook to discuss further what to expect if we decide to have Ray taken off of the artificial nutrition and hydration. I was going to ask to leave work early, but first I had to talk to my supervisor about what had transpired between the time I left work on Friday and today.

"Charlene, can I talk to you privately?" I asked. "It's about Ray."

"Okay, let's go in the conference room," she said. "I should bring tissues shouldn't I?"

I nodded, holding back tears. We went to the conference room and shut the door. I got through everything with just a tiny tear trickling down my cheek. Charlene didn't fair as well. She kept wiping her face.

I told her, "I don't know what will happen once they take away the artificial nutrition. I don't know how long it will take for him to pass."

She assured me that I could take off whatever time I needed. I made it through that conversation with a calmness that surprised me.

"That wasn't so bad, was it?" I asked Charlene. She nodded, as she wiped her cheeks one more time. "It'll be okay," I said. "He'll be going off to heaven, where he'll be happy."

There I was again, comforting someone and assuring them that everything was going to be okay. If I say it enough, maybe it will be.

One hurdle conquered today, then on to the next. If I get any more, I'll fall flat on my face, literally. I left work early after the meeting was coordinated with my sister, my parents, the chaplain of Northbrook, the social worker, Emily, the head nurse on Ray's floor, Nancy, and Dr. Patel. We met in a tiny office on Ray's floor. Lynn was meeting everyone for the first time. She hadn't been in to see Ray yet. My parents knew only the head nurse on Ray's floor, Nancy. I knew everyone but the chaplain. His name was Rob O'Shay. He was of slight build, with kind eyes and a voice to match. Oh, how I needed kind words at that moment.

Now was the time to ask any questions before we made the final decision to have Ray withdrawn from the artificial nutrition.

He could be kept in Northbrook or be taken care of by Hospice. With Hospice, he couldn't be on any IV medication.

"How will he be getting his anti-seizure medication?" I wanted to know. He couldn't get it orally. "If he doesn't get it, he'll have seizures. That would be a horrible way to go." Everyone agreed.

Okay, so Ray would stay in Northbrook and receive what they call comfort care. They would take him off of his artificial nutrition and hydration, and give him pain meds and his anti-seizure medication, until he passed away naturally. When we talked about how long it would take for Ray to pass, Dad started crying. I've never seen him cry, ever, not in my whole entire life. All of this time he had been strong or putting up a good front.

I had one more question that had been nagging at me all weekend. "Why didn't West End tell us how grave Raymond was?" I asked. "They led us to believe that the holes in his stomach were going to heal, and that he was going to have a new feeding tube put in."

Dr. Patel shook her head back and forth. "They do that to us all the time," she said. "They patch people up and send them to us to deal with."

I wondered if other hospitals did that, also, to keep their death statistics low. If they get the patients out before they die, it won't be a black spot on their record. It may make them look good, but it's cruel to mislead the family like we were misled.

We had all of our questions answered, and we needed to talk to the rest of our family before we made our final decision. We would meet again with Dr. Patel tomorrow to discuss what our family wanted.

Once our meeting was over, Rob O'Shay corralled us to give us words of consolation. He made his way down the hall, walking with a cane. So, he had suffered through a few hard times, himself.

"You can call me any time that you want to talk," he told us. I made a note of that because I would just love to talk to him.

Raymond needed to be taken to West End Hospital to have a second PICC line put in. From what I gather, he needs one to give him his artificial nutrition and hydration, and one to administer his meds. Now he'll have one in each arm. After the meeting, we went to Ray's room, only to find him being loaded onto a gurney to be taken in an ambulance to the hospital. Both ambulance attendants were on the side of the bed away from the window trying to get Ray out of the bed. Ray was holding on to the bed railing on the window side of the bed. He would not let go.

Emily had to squeeze past the attendants and between the bed and the window. "Now, Raymond, you have to let go," she gently chastised him. She pried his hand off of the railing, and he let out a yelp of glee.

The attendants put Ray on the gurney and wheeled him down the hall. Ray grinned from ear to ear as he was whisked by us. One attendant jokingly said to him, "Raymond, why don't you cheer up a little?" I never knew anyone who was in the hospital for as long as Ray and was as ill as Ray who still had a smile left in him.

I tried to remember that smile because once they withdrew Ray's artificial nutrition, I knew I wouldn't be seeing it for more than a few short weeks, if that long.

January 31, Tuesday

I had to leave work early again after a meeting was coordinated with Dr. Patel, Emily the social worker, Lynn, my parents, and me to discuss our final decision to take Ray off of his artificial nutrition and hydration.

We were to meet in the dining room and TV area on Ray's floor. Emily, Lynn, Mom, Dad, and I sat around a large round table, talking about getting a TV for Ray, who would bring in his clothes, where to get food, and so on. This went on for about 15 minutes, until I finally asked Emily, "When are we going to speak to Dr. Patel?"

"About what?" she asked.

"What do you mean, about what? About taking Ray off of his artificial nutrition," I said.

Emily put her hands on both cheeks, and said, "Oh, that's a whole other ball game. Let me go get Dr. Patel." She rushed out of the room to get the doctor.

A sinking feeling of foreboding crept into my stomach. The doctor came quickly, and plopped herself down next to me. She wasn't looking any of us in the eye.

"Your family can't make the decision to take Ray off of his artificial nutrition. Your parents are not Ray's guardians," she told us.

"What?" I exclaimed. I looked at my parents hoping for an explanation.

My mom offered one. "I assumed that we were," she said. "We were asked to make decisions on everything. Why wouldn't we be our son's guardian?"

There we go again with the questions. Why were there always more questions than answers? "Who is Ray's guardian?" I asked.

"Raymond doesn't have a guardian. He is a ward of the state, but he was never appointed a guardian. We assumed that your parents were the guardians," Dr. Patel answered.

She made some sort of apology and left us alone to assimilate the news that we were bombarded with and what the implications of Ray not having a guardian meant. Of course, we had no idea what it meant. We weren't attorneys or law-makers or employees of the NYS DDSO.

Stunned yet again, we left Northbrook to make our way home. Later that day, we were told that Dr. O'Conner, the director of medical services of Northbrook, was going to examine Raymond and make recommendations. We were hopeful again. We knew that once he saw how bad Ray was, he would recommend to Northbrook's ethics board—which reviews requests to take people off of life support— that Ray's artificial nutrition should be taken out.

February 1, Wednesday

The call came from Emily of Northbrook. She said, "Your father asked me to call you and convey to you what Dr. O'Conner found." If my parents didn't want to call me, I knew it wasn't going to be good. "Dr. O'Conner said that when he saw Ray, he was smiling and responding. He has quality of life. He can respond to your family. He recommends that we leave everything as it is for now."

"What does that mean? You're going to keep him on IVs indefinitely? I was told that you should only keep them in for three months. Then what happens?" I asked.

"Let me have you speak to Nancy," Emily said. I was transferred to Nancy. She repeated again what Dr. O'Conner said.

"So, basically we're going to watch him wither away. What happens after three months if he's still alive?" I asked.

"Well, maybe that won't happen. Often times they develop septic," Nancy said.

I asked, "So, they're keeping him alive until he gets sick?"

"Well, until we come to another road."

"Like him getting septic. What is that?" I asked.

"It's an infection in the blood."

"Does he suffer?" I asked.

"We'll make sure that he doesn't suffer."

"And if his stomach heals, are they going to put him back into West End, and try to put in another feeding tube that they can't guarantee will work, and have him go through this all over again?" I asked.

No answer to that question.

"He won't go back to West End," Nancy said. "He'll go to Michael Fitzsimmons Hospital."

Who gives a flying fig where he goes, if it gets to that point? I wanted to yell into the phone. Raymond has suffered enough, and it needs to stop. I had to calm myself down. There was not a thing that I could do to end this nightmare. Or was there? I didn't know who to turn to for help.

Once I calmed down enough to have a conversation without my voice shaking from anger, I called my parents' house. Mom answered. I forgot that I wasn't going to discuss Raymond with her. "I'm going to talk to the director of Northbrook," I blurted out.

"Why?" she asked.

"Because none of this should have happened to us, Mom. This never should have happened," I replied. We never should have been asked to make such a gut-wrenching decision about a loved one and then be told that our wishes couldn't be honored because the state didn't have a guardian appointed for Raymond. The anger began festering inside me again. Why wasn't my mother upset by any of this?

"How are you going to talk to her?" she asked me.

"Her name is on the list of contacts that Emily gave us. It's right at the top of the list: Norma Jean Smythe of administration. I'm going to call her office and ask to speak to her," I said. I knew that my mom wasn't too keen on the idea, but I didn't care. I hung up and called the phone number on the list.

"Can I speak to Norma Jean Smythe?" I asked the woman who answered.

"Can I ask why?" she inquired. I told her what had happened with my brother.

"Hold on. I'll put you through," she said.

Norma Jean came on the phone, and told me that her hands were tied. Ray was under the NYS DDSO and the state, which mandated that every person has the right to nutrition. I prefer to talk about emotional issues face to face rather than on the phone, so I asked if I could speak to her in person. "I had a meeting that was cancelled, so I have the rest of the afternoon off. When can you come down?" she asked.

"I can be there in 20 minutes," I replied. I hadn't asked my supervisor if I could leave early, but, hey, she said that I could take off any time I needed to deal with what was happening to Ray. She gave me no problem at all.

Within 20 minutes, I was sitting across the desk from Norma Jean Smythe, a fortyish- looking woman, very simply dressed, and a little gruff in her mannerisms. She immediately put me at ease with her responsiveness. She at first tried to appease me. "I can assure you that Ray's case manager has his best interests at heart," she said.

"Oh, the one who is so sure that Ray's going to heal, so they can put a tube back in his stomach and send him back to the group home?" I asked her.

She had no response to this. I know I wasn't being fair to Joe, but I was so incensed at what was happening with Ray.

Then she said, "The group home is also concerned with Ray's care."

"The group home that put him in the hospital and didn't arrange for someone to be with him in the 3½ weeks he was there, and promised that it wouldn't happen again? The one who sent him back to West End in a condition so bad that they said he may not make it there?" I said to her.

She just looked down at her desk. There was silence from her. I imagine that didn't happen very often.

I told her, "I'm not going to fight the decision by Dr. O'Conner, if that's what you're concerned about." She seemed relieved.

"What would happen if we got guardianship of Ray?" I asked her.

"Then you could make that decision," she replied. She meant the decision to take Ray off of the artificial nutrition.

"I heard that getting guardianship was a long, drawn-out procedure," I said.

"I've seen it take one day and I've seen it take months," she said. "You know, we are just as confused as you are. We thought that your parents were Ray's guardians, too. West End insisted that your parents were Ray's guardians."

No big surprise there. Look at how they screwed up so much when Ray was there.

Then Norma Jean started shaking her head. "We don't like taking wards of the state anymore, because we have so many problems dealing with the state."

I wished that she could have told me what happened to make her facility dislike dealing with the state so much, but I knew that she wasn't allowed to tell me. Health care facilities can't make things like that public because of the privacy laws, so lawmakers aren't held to task when the laws they pass or don't pass cause such inhumane conditions. The only way that the public can know such things is if people like my family speak out.

I thanked the director for her time, patience, and truthfulness, then went out to the lobby to call Mike. He didn't know that I had left work early.

"I think I'm going to look into getting guardianship," I announced to Mike.

"Then you'll be responsible for all of his bills," he said.

"How do you know that?" I asked.

"We'll ask Matt," he suggested.

"How does he know?"

"Well, he's an attorney."

"Well, I know attorneys through work who don't know squat, and screw their clients."

"Pat, he's a friend. He's not going to screw us," Mike said.

I knew that, but my mind wasn't able to rationalize at that moment.

"I'll ask your sister, Katherine," I said. She has worked as an assistant to attorneys for years.

Mike could sense that there was no reasoning with me, so he let me vent.

"All I know is that this has been wrong from the very beginning, and I have to do something about it," I told him.

Oh, how I wish that I could pass this burden on to someone else. I wish that I could just pay an attorney to handle everything, like talking to people, trying to investigate why things are so screwed up, anything so I didn't have to fight with people anymore. I knew that wasn't possible. I wasn't going to be released from my turmoil.

Mike and I said our goodbyes, and I went up to Ray's room. Ray was trying to roll over, but he couldn't quite make it. I tried helping him, but he wouldn't let me. He was so agitated. He kept opening his eyes and staring blankly into space. Then he rolled his eyes upward into his head, and went back to sleep. This is the quality of life that Dr. O'Conner says Ray has.

Ray slept the whole time I was there, except for the few times that he rolled and yelled. A blonde nurse named Laura came in once when he did this. I informed her, "It seems like he's uncomfortable, like he's in pain or something."

"Do you want me to give him pain medicine?" she asked. "You said that he hasn't had any since 11:00?"

"Yes," I replied.

"I've been trying to hold off because he didn't seem to be in pain," she said.

We rolled Ray to his left side, the one that he likes best, and he still was yelling out, that half-growl and half-yell that he makes with his mouth wide open. Something was bothering him. Laura went out to get Ray's pain medicine, while I held his hand and rubbed it. He went back to sleep.

Laura returned with a needle. "Do you want me to disturb him?" she asked. I didn't know.

"Well, he doesn't have any muscles left, but we give it subcutaneously," she said. That means just under the skin. She pulled the covers back. I could see her looking for a spot on Ray's emaciated body, somewhere that still had some meat. There wasn't any spot like that anymore.

"Well, let's try his butt," she said, with a grimace. "I don't want to hurt him." As she was injecting the medicine into his bony behind, I watched Ray's face. He never flinched, never opened his eyes, never moved. He slept blissfully through being poked with a needle. "I think he's so used to being poked that it doesn't even faze him anymore," I assured Laura.

I knelt down on the floor next to Ray's bed, and held his hand. When I relaxed my grip, he woke up and grabbed it back. All he wanted was his zebra and a hand to hold.

I cried. "Poor honey, I tried, I tried, I really tried. I'm sorry, Ray-Ray. I don't know what to do to help you," I told him.

I didn't get a single one of his beautiful smiles today. When I left him, he was curled up in a fetal position, hugging his big stuffed zebra that must have been brought in by Joe Griffin from Ray's group home. Ray's face was hidden from the world that was keeping him artificially alive.

February 2, Thursday

I can't concentrate on my work. I keep breaking down crying. I just learned of a little eight-year-old girl who was a ward of the state. She was unconscious and on a respirator. Her heart kept stopping. The facility had to keep resuscitating her, because she didn't have a guardian to sign a do-not-resuscitate order on her behalf. How can lawmakers allow that to happen to a helpless little girl? Raymond's predicament is not an isolated incident. I'll bet that tragic scenarios like Raymond's are happening all over New York State, but we aren't hearing about them because the victims can't talk.

I called my psychiatrist for tranquilizers. She won't prescribe them unless she sees me. I have an appointment to see her tomorrow.

I called my dad to tell him that I'll take the TV that he had at his house to Raymond's room. The nursing home doesn't provide one, and poor Ray has been lying in his room for days without a room-mate, any music, or even a TV to provide a distraction.

"It's not that heavy, Dad," I said.

"No, I can take it," he said. My dad doesn't like to ask his daughters to do anything. He thinks he's bothering us. I don't know where he gets that idea from. I don't mind helping him at all.

"Dad, you have fractured ribs," I reminded him.

"That's okay. I'll put that belt thing on," he replied.

I'm worried about my dad. He seems to be so fragile lately; or has he been getting like this and I just haven't noticed until now? I can see when Dad walks that his towering frame doesn't move as steadily as it used to.

"Dad, I can carry it. It's not that heavy," I said. How was I going to get him to allow me to take the TV to Ray's room?

After I hung up, I thought, darn it, Ray has a TV at his group home, the home that's supposed to be looking after his best interests. They can bring his TV. The state is the one keeping him alive. The least they could do is get a TV for Ray.

I called my parents back and spoke to my mom, "Mom, if the group home cared, they should have someone bring Ray's TV to him. Ray's in a room all by himself with no stimulation."

"They probably don't know that," Mom replied.

"Mom, Joe Griffin knows that. He's been to see Ray. Emily said that he was there. He knows, Mom. He knows," I said.

Mom called the group home, and then called me back. Ray would have his TV by Saturday. Why, if we have no rights, do we always have to be looking after Ray's best interests? I can't even think of what would be happening to Ray if he had no family to look after him. What happens to the people in group homes who have been abandoned by their families?

My brother from Georgia called me at work to offer support. I started crying into the phone. He said he would come into town if I needed him.

Everyone is offering support except the people who have control. I'm going to do something to make sure that no one has to go through what my family and Ray have, but I don't know what.

Before I went to Ray's room today, I stopped at the nurses' station and asked for Nancy, but she wasn't in and wouldn't be in until tomorrow. A tall, stunning black woman, whose name tag identified her as a nurse practitioner, asked me if I had any concerns that she could help me with.

I told her, "Yesterday I came in, and my brother was rolling in bed and growling like he was in pain. This was at 6:00. He hadn't had any pain medication since 11:00 in the morning. I just want to make sure that it doesn't happen again."

A nurse, who was new to the floor, said, "All he has to do is ask."

"He can't talk," I said.

Another nurse at the nurses' station said, "He makes noises when he's uncomfortable, and we give him his meds then."

So what if he doesn't make any noise? He doesn't get pain meds? Until that moment I had great confidence in the facility. Was he going to be ignored, like at West End? The nurse practitioner said that she would address the problem.

Later, the same nurse practitioner came down to Ray's room. She asked me questions about how long Ray was crippled up and about his neurological disorders. I tried to remember every ailment that he had. Out of the blue she said, "So, we have a Terry Schiavo case here."

While Raymond was in West End, I took an interest in the Terry Schiavo case and read up on it. I promised that I wouldn't go to the press with Raymond's case because my family didn't want to be surrounded by reporters and have demonstrations like in Terry Schiavo's final days. We didn't want our personal struggle to be on public display.

Terry Schiavo's case had completely different circumstances. Different state. Different laws.

I said, "No, that was different. That was the families fighting over Terry Schiavo's right to die. Our family is all in agreement. We want to let Ray go. It's the state that won't let Ray go."

"That's unusual," she replied. "Usually, it's the family fighting. So, now it will go before the ethics board."

"No. We were told that we have no rights. That's it. Besides, Dr. O'Conner has seen Ray and made a decision. He says that Ray has quality of life," I said.

"Usually it's the family that won't let go. Well, that's just something I heard," she said.

They were talking about us, I thought to myself. I bet the whole facility is discussing Ray and his plight. I'd be talking, too, if I worked there.

"How often does Dr. O'Conner see Ray?" I asked.

"Oh, he won't see him again," she replied.

So, he had made his decision based on seeing Ray once for a few minutes. "I'm just asking because when he saw Ray, he was smiling and reacting. For the past two days, Ray has been like this, lethargic and sleeping most of the time. I'd like him to see Ray like this," I said.

"Well, I'll discuss it with Dr. Patel, and she can talk with Dr. O'Conner," she replied.

"Oh, I don't think that will work," I said. "She's the one who asked us to consider comfort care, and he overrode her." There's no hope. We have to watch Ray wither away. This is what they call quality of life.

I had dinner at Mom's and Dad's house. My dad made pot pie. Homemade pot pie. The only thing that makes me feel any better lately is stuffing my face with comfort food. I know that I'm packing on the pounds, but I don't care. I'll deal with that later.

While we were sitting in the living room, I talked to Mom because it was bothering me what Lynn had told me earlier today. "Mom, Lynn said that you were relieved by Dr. O'Conner's decision," I said. "If you weren't comfortable with our decision to take Ray off that artificial nutrition and to let him pass, why didn't you say anything? We all agreed that if anyone wasn't comfortable with taking the IV away from Ray, that we would honor that person's wishes and we wouldn't fight over it. Why didn't you say anything?"

"Well, I'd feel guilty if I was the one deciding to take Ray's life," she said.

That's why my mother wasn't upset when Dr. O'Connor said Ray had quality of life.

I was talking about Ray with one of Mike's cousins earlier in the week, and she said the same thing, "I couldn't do that. I couldn't decide to pull the plug on someone."

I will never understand how you could watch someone suffer needlessly when you know that they're going to die anyway. It's not like we want to euthanize Ray. We're just taking away artificial life support that's only prolonging Ray's suffering and letting him pass naturally.

Well, Mom expressed her concern. I was thinking of fighting Dr. O'Conner's decision by going for guardianship, but now I couldn't do anything. I had to honor her wishes, even though deep in my heart I didn't agree with them.

February 3, Friday

Today I'm too tired to be angry. The only emotion I have is all-consuming sorrow.

I left work in the middle of the day to see my psychiatrist. I've been on medication for years for depression, but it's been under control. I normally have to see my psychiatrist every six months to renew my prescriptions, but I wanted to get something temporary, some mild sedative, to calm my jangled nerves. I'm still getting pains in my chest. I've had the same pains before, though, and numerous tests revealed absolutely nothing. I wanted to get a sedative to see if my pains were just muscle spasms. If the pains continued while I was on the sedatives, then I would go to a heart doctor.

Sitting in my psychiatrist's office, I told her about the passing away of my father-in-law and my sister-in-law, and then my brother's ordeal. She was all sympathetic and wrote out a script for an anti-anxiety medication. It was so potent, that she advised me to try one tablet. If it was too strong, I was to break it into halves. If it was still too strong, I was to break it into quarters.

As my psychiatrist and I were walking down the hall once my visit was over, she turned to me, handed me the prescription, and said, "How tragic, but, you know, you have to be stronger. Think of what your mother is going through." With that, she turned and went back to her office. Wow, her sudden lack of empathy astounded me.

Well, she made me stop crying. When I'm mad, I don't cry. I went back to work to finish my day with great indignation that my psychiatrist would be so callous.

My friend, Ginny, came up to see how I was. "Pat, why did you come back to work?" she asked. "You should have gone home."

"No, I'm okay Ginny. I have to save my time. I don't know how much time I'll have to take off when Ray gets really bad," I replied.

I really wasn't okay, but the uncertainty of what will happen to Ray makes me keep going into work, even though I'm not of much use in my state of mind.

Lynn called me after she went to see Ray. She said that she sat in the dark, crying. She couldn't look at Ray's face. It was contorted in such misery. The nurse finally gave Ray his pain medication, but it took about 15 minutes for it to start taking effect. Lynn then went out to the nurses' station and talked to the nurse. Ray was getting his pain meds between every five to seven hours. Lynn told them that Ray needed more.

The nurse on duty said, "Well, we don't like to give him too much. It might do something to him." Like what? Kill him? That would be a blessing. The nurse contacted the doctor on call and had Ray's pain prescription upped to every 4 hours. He's also getting high doses of aspirin when he has a fever or when the pain meds don't seem to be doing the trick.

The IV tower next to Ray's bed has two monitors to administer his IVs. It also has so many bags and tubes between his artificial nutrition and his medications, that I don't know how the nurses keep everything straight. I'd love to know how much Ray's treatment is costing Medicaid. I'd love to know how many other families in New York State are suffering the same fate as ours. What a waste — physically, mentally and monetarily such a waste.

Ray haunts me even when I don't see him. Before I got the call from Lynn, I hadn't cried for, oh, a few hours. The tears gushed out uncontrolled all over again. I had to get a grip. I had to go pick up my anti-anxiety medicine at the pharmacy.

Paul came home after a party tonight, stinking drunk. He said that he didn't drive his car, but didn't know who brought it home. Mike came into the room where I was resting in my recliner to try to tell me what condition Paul had returned home in. I was too groggy from taking my tranquilizer to care. I faintly lifted up my head and asked, "Can we talk about this tomorrow?" Then I plopped my head back down on the arm of the recliner I was sprawled out in.

Poor Mike, his son was in his bedroom in a drunken stupor, and his wife was passed out in the recliner from a drugged stupor.

The tranquilizers are too much for me at full dose. I'll have to take a quarter-dose next time.

February 4, Saturday

I woke up today, thinking I might be wrong about Ray-Ray not surviving much longer. Then I went to see him. My parents were in Ray's room when I got there. They said that they were with Ray just before it came down to the time for his medicine. He was in pain and yelling. They had to go to the nurses' station to beg them to give the injection a few minutes earlier. The controlled medicines are locked up, so they can't be administered at just any old time someone wants them. It took awhile before the nurse came to the room to give Ray his injection. Now my mom is upset. She said that she's going to call Dr. O'Conner. I don't think that she'll be forceful enough. I don't think her little body has the energy anymore to be forceful.

I want to sit on the director of Northbrook's doorstep until she talks to me. The director lied to me. She assured me that Ray wouldn't suffer and that Dr. O'Conner is a compassionate man. Liars, the bunch of them are.

My parents left to go home. It was after dinner when the aides came to change Raymond. This time they didn't shut the door to the room when they cleaned him up. I stood in the doorway and saw the two holes in Ray's abdomen. I saw his stomach juices ooze out when he moved. The aides saw me put my hand over my mouth. I felt like I was going to wretch. I had to leave the room and walk down the hallway to the window I stare out of when Ray's plight is too much for me to bear. Somehow, it calms me to see that there is a normal world outside and that it's still going on despite the turmoil in my little world.

Today I wasn't settled down looking out that window. Ray's bony body was stuck in my mind. He's looking more and more like the concentration camp people when they liberated Germany. They received good, compassionate care after their liberation. Raymond will have no liberation until they are compassionate enough to let him pass.

When the aides were done, one of them came out into the hall. "We're done. Are you okay?" I was asked. What if I wasn't? Would they give me drugs or something? I just said yes to make things easier.

Ray isn't peaceful today. Even when he's sleeping, he moves his head from side to side as if he's having nightmares. Why won't God take him so that he can be at peace? Supposedly everyone is looking after Ray's best interests. The people here are doing the best that they can, but their hands are tied by state laws. The anger is seething in me, yet again. My emotions are on a roller-coaster course. Today

I want revenge for what is happening to Ray. I may not get it now, but some day, some day I will get revenge.

February 5, Sunday

Ray-Ray, he's always on my mind. While I took a bath, I decided that I will sue the state for negligence. I don't know how to go about it, but I'll find out. Poor Ray-Ray is a ward of the state, and they are supposed to be looking after him. As far as I can see, my family and I are the only ones making sure that he is taken care of. Oh, the state checks on his doctors and his treatment, but his everyday care they don't have a clue about, because they don't have anyone watching him hour after hour, like we do. If we have no rights, why are we the ones who have to ask for him to get his pain meds more often? If we have no rights, why are my parents always asked to sign forms giving consent for treatment? I go round and round with this. Who is responsible for what and who isn't, and I get no real answers.

When Paul woke up this afternoon, I gave him a lecture about drinking. I told him that I'm not naïve about drinking, that I myself have gotten so drunk that I don't remember what I did. It scared the crap out of me to be so out of control, and I never got that drunk again.

"I'm not saying that I never drank again," I told him, "but I always made sure that I was staying where I was at or that a responsible person would be taking me home if I drank too much. Paul, you don't know that the person who drove you home wasn't drinking. You don't even know who drove you home." Paul just stood and said nothing. "I couldn't bear it if something happened to you or any of your friends," I said. My voice cracked.

I ended the conversation with, "Paul, I'm just saying this to you because I love you," and I hugged him. Each hug, each lecture, each, "I love you" is filled with more emotion than it used to be. I think tragedy makes you focus on what's really important. Saying "I love you" every chance I get is at the top of my list.

Lynn called me and said that when she got to Northbrook, Ray was sitting in his wheelchair at the nurses' station, smiling away. The only reason that I can figure out for his complete change from yesterday to today is that he probably wasn't sleeping because he was in such pain. And today, since they had been giving him his meds every four hours, he was finally able to sleep soundly.

I'm glad he's doing better, but this doesn't solve our dilemma. What will be done if Raymond survives past the three-month time limit that doctors state PICC lines should be used? Do we just have to wait for him to become septic, or get pneumonia, or something else God-awful? What will time bring? In my wildest dreams, I couldn't have imagined the situation that we all are in now. I don't want to imagine what nightmare will be around the corner.

February 6, Monday

I was so tired at work that I had to hold my head up with my hands. I think that I did doze off for a minute or two. My co-workers wouldn't have said anything. They'd have just let me sleep.

I went to see Ray today. Lynn and I feel safe enough at Northbrook to visit Ray alone, so we are splitting up the weekdays that we visit him. We're going after work, bringing something for dinner, and staying as late as we can. We're also staying longer on Saturday or Sunday so that we can each, including Mom and Dad, have a weekend day off from seeing Ray. My parents' health isn't great, and this whole thing with Ray is draining them. I'm half their age, and I'm exhausted. I'm still working full-time and trying to take care of my family, along with Ray.

I'm not complaining. I never mind one minute spent with Ray. When I'm in the room with him, it's like the rest of the world doesn't exist. I hold his hand, or play toss with his stuffed animals, or sing to him, or just talk. He's a great listener when he's not sleeping. I find myself talking to him a lot.

I think that at times he actually understood what I was telling him. Sometimes he'd look at me with the same intensity that my son did as an infant. It was as if he was taking in every word I said and analyzing what I was saying. It would be just for a fleeting moment, like his soul was looking at my soul through his eyes. In an instant, it would be gone. Then Ray's eyes would sparkle with laughter, and he'd throw his zebra at me.

For entertainment, I pop a tape into his TV—usually *The Sound of Music* or some cartoon. Sometimes I bring in my laptop and put it on his moveable bed-stand. That way, I can bring it close to him, and he can see it better. Today we watched almost the entire TV series of *The Beverly Hillbillies*. It was just me holding Ray's hand while he was hugging his big stuffed zebra.

For some reason, Raymond didn't have a blanket today, just a sheet. His feet were cold. His usual nurse at night, Laura, got a blanket for me. Ray gets extra special attention from her when she's on duty. She pops her head in every time she walks by the room to see if we need anything. On one of her trips past Ray's room, she asked me, "Have you talked to Emily about guardianship?"

I answered, "She said that she didn't think it was a good idea, but I didn't get a chance to ask her why." I asked Laura where I could find a copy of the law that was keeping Ray alive much longer than he should be. I was told that the social worker would look into getting me a copy.

At least I saw Ray smile today, but his smile is so weak. I can see a difference in Ray in just a week. He seems to have lost his will to live. His hands aren't in constant motion anymore. All he wants to do is hold my hand. He has a low-grade fever—100 degrees. It's horrible, but I hope that whatever is causing the fever takes him, so he doesn't linger.

Before I left for the night, I pulled the blanket up over Ray and tucked him in. I broke down, crying. I felt like I was covering up my own baby. "I'm sorry, Ray-Ray. I can't help you. I'm so sorry," I apologize to him every time I see him.

I had gone the whole day without crying until that moment. I had to leave, but my heart wants to stay. The staff, by now, is used to seeing me walk down the hall to the elevator dabbing the tears away from my cheeks.

February 7, Tuesday

For some reason, my mom and dad have to go to West End Hospital to sign a consent form to have Ray's PICC line replaced. It had clogged. Why do they have to keep doing that if Ray is a ward of the state and the family has no rights? I asked Emily that once, and she just shook her head in bewilderment.

I called my mom and asked her why she's going to the hospital. I said, "Mom, why are you doing the state's job?"

"I don't know, Pat. I just want him taken care of," she replied.

"Mom you're not his guardian. Isn't it illegal for you to give consent?" I asked. No answer from Mom. I pressed on. "I think I'll call the director of all the group homes in this area. His name is on the top of that correspondence from Joe Griffin," I said.

"Why would you call him?" she asked.

"Because, Mom, this is wrong," I replied. "This whole thing has been a mess from the very beginning. Mom, this shouldn't be happening."

"Pat, you're letting yourself get too upset," she said.

"Someone has to get upset, Mom. Someone has to," I said. "You know what's upsetting me? The fact that no one is getting upset about what's happening to Ray. That's what's upsetting me."

I know that she was just trying to get me to calm down so I didn't have a heart attack or a stroke or something. She's been dealing with Ray's ailments for 54 years. He's almost died several times, so she was used to seeing her son gravely ill. But, still, I didn't understand how she could be so calm through all of this—or was I overreacting? I feel so many emotions, that they gush forth without my being able to control them anymore. I hope that everyone forgives me when this is all over, especially my mother.

I contemplated taking pictures and a video of Ray. I want Ray's story told, but I have to wait until Ray has passed so that we can mourn in private. We don't want the right-to-lifers getting involved or to be hounded by reporters. They can be so heartless at times. I don't want them to be sticking their microphones in our faces and asking us, "How do you feel?" Then I'd be compelled to blurt out, "How the bleep-bleep do you think I feel?"

Emily is trying to arrange a meeting on Friday with all of the parties involved in Ray's care. I think that it may have been the group home or the state that asked for it to be arranged. Lynn asked Emily if Dr. O'Conner will be present. Emily said, "I'll try to get him there. The meeting has to be in the afternoon because your dad has an appointment in the morning." My parents have so many doctors' appointments. It seems like every week one of them is going to a doctor for something.

Lynn left, and I just sat and held Ray's hand. My religion has taught me that every person has a soul that is a whole being even though the body may be broken, like Raymond's. I read in a spiritual book that even when a person is unconscious their soul can still hear what you say.

While Raymond slept, I decided to talk to his soul. "I know that you don't understand me, but I know that your soul is in there somewhere, Ray-Ray. It's okay to go. Your angels will take care of you. Heaven is more beautiful than you could ever imagine, and you can run, Ray-Ray. You can run as much as you want. Our sister Janet is waiting for you. You don't have to be afraid. We won't leave you alone, and when you get to the other side, all your angels will be there to help you. You just need to stop fighting."

I sat for a long, long time, just rubbing Ray's hand and contemplating what I was going to do about what is happening to him. I'm over my anger for now. Well, for today, anyway. Now I'm just going to get even. Not today, not tomorrow, but I will get even.

February 8, Wednesday

Today is my friend Ginny's birthday. I went out last night and bought some fleece at the fabric store, finished off the edges to make a blanket, and wrapped it for a present for Ginny. I also wanted to make a nice, bright blanket for Ray-Ray. I found a psychedelic-looking print with the words "love," "joy," and "peace" in bright colors of green, red, blue, and yellow. I don't know if he'll appreciate it, but it'll brighten up his room of beige walls and metal furniture. I can't wait to give it to him. Tired as I was, it felt good to be thinking about something else besides Ray's misery.

Yesterday I thought that I was exhausted, but today was even worse. I hit a terrible slump in the late afternoon; then by 4:00 my angels must have given me a jolt of energy.

Lynn called me at work to tell me the time of the meeting with the people involved in Ray's care. Lynn told me, "Emily sent you a letter about the meeting. She handed Mom and Dad a letter yesterday. I don't think Northbrook has my address, do they?"

"Come to think of it, no, I don't remember putting your name or address on any of the forms I filled out," I said. "I got mad at Mom yesterday."

"Yeah, she said something about you being upset," Lynn responded.

"I just don't understand why she doesn't want me to talk to anyone. I guess that everyone handles stress in their own way. I get rid of my stress by doing something about whatever is wrong. Mom has her own way of dealing with stress. I'll call her and apologize for getting mad at her. I want us all to be talking to each other on Friday. We have to put up a united front."

Today when I walked the stairs alone in the building where I work, the picture of Mom crying over Ray and him patting her hand on his 50th birthday popped into my head. What am I thinking? Mom cares about Ray. She's been fighting for him for 54 years, and she's tired. It's time for someone else to fight. I guess that someone else is me.

I continued to walk the stairs because physical activity consumes the energy that feeds my anxiety. I climbed the stairs and cried and prayed to anyone and everyone in heaven who would listen. I asked them to tell me what to do about Raymond. I wanted them to take Ray from his world of misery. I wanted this to never happen to anyone else ever again.

How will I accomplish that? I asked for a sign. Do I sue the state? Do I take Ray's story to the newspaper? Do I write my own story? Do I try for guardianship? Oh, my God. Ray haunts me so. I don't know who is responsible for this whole sad mess. I may never know.

When I was exhausted, I went back to work.

Today Ray-Ray was worse than I've ever seen him. The look on his face was pure, utter misery. He was whimpering. He no longer had the strength to yell or roll over by himself. He was burning up. I went to the nurse and asked if he had a fever. The nurse took Ray's temperature. It was 104. No wonder he was so weak. The poor thing didn't want much. He kept grabbing my hand. I sat for hours by his side. He wasn't even hugging his stuffed zebra today. How could anyone make one of God's children suffer needlessly like this?

I rubbed Ray's head until he fell asleep. Oh, how I wanted to stay with him. He's just a baby in a man's body. With a heavy heart I snuck out of his room without waking him. I prayed that God would make him sleep through the night so he wouldn't wake up sick and alone in the dark.

When I got home, I called my mother to apologize. She wasn't upset at all about our last phone conversation. I think this whole ordeal is making both of us a little wacky. Okay, I made amends so that we could all go in on Friday with clear heads. I can't think straight with anger and hurt in my head.

Mom thinks that Dr. O'Conner is the one who is making Ray stay alive, and I don't think that's the case. It's this law that the state has that mentally retarded people can only have court-appointed guardians make end-of-life decisions, but doesn't make provisions for automatically appointing guardians. How did the state laws get so screwed up? Too often it's the people who can't speak up for themselves who suffer the most because of governmental policies.

I think that my mother is in for a rude awakening. I think she assumes the meeting on Friday will end Ray's suffering, and I think she's wrong. I don't think the staff at Northbrook will find a way around the laws. I don't think our dilemma will be solved easily.

February 9, Thursday

I'm tired beyond anything I've ever felt. I say that every day when I wake up, and every day somehow I make it through. I have a cold, and my exhaustion is suffocating me. My mind is going in so many directions at once; and I can't concentrate on anything anymore.

I just might get a reprieve tonight. Lynn is going to see Ray. She can only see him until 5:00 PM. If he's bad, I'll go see him after her.

Paul wrote a note to me today. It read: "Please, please, please if there is any dinner to be had, please save me some tonight, as I have no means of obtaining food." He's 20 years old. He has some money. We have food in the house, just not food that he can find. Well, maybe there isn't food. I can't remember the last time that I did any grocery shopping.

Mike sees my exhaustion, but he's busy with tax season. In a rare moment, when we had time to sit together and eat dinner, he suggested that we get someone to clean the house on a weekly basis. I could use that, but I also need someone who will fold clothes and put them away. I need someone who will put dirty dishes in the dishwasher and unload it. I need someone who will make lunches and get my clothes ready for work. I need a couple days of doing nothing. None of this will happen. It's only an exhausted woman's delusions.

Mike offered to go grocery shopping for me. Maybe I'll get a full night's sleep tonight so that I can think clearly at the meeting at Northbrook tomorrow. Mary, my oldest sister, is coming in from Pennsylvania for the meeting. Personally, I think that we'll get absolutely nothing done. It's a waste of time. This whole fiasco will continue. Maybe I'll be wrong. Maybe a miracle will happen, and we will get some answers. I pray and pray and pray that God will intervene and give us some peace, whatever that will entail.

Ray had a raging fever of 104 yesterday. Today it's gone. Lynn left me an e-mail message tonight saying that.

February 10, Friday

The meeting at Northbrook took place promptly at 11:30 AM. I finally met face to face with Dr. O'Conner, Amy, the director of the group home, and Joe Griffin. They all sat around a long table, along with Nancy, Emily, Chaplain O'Shay, Dr. Patel, my parents, my sisters, and me. I was ready for a fight about the quality of life I've seen in Ray over the past two weeks. I started to say, "You talked about quality of life. My quality of life with my brother is to hold his hand while he…"

A slightly built Dr. O'Conner suddenly interrupted, as soon as Emily acknowledged that everyone was in the room except for the doctor from the NYS DDSO. "We're not going to discuss quality of life for Ray," he said. "We're talking about Ray's medical condition. He has a fissure, if that is still draining. He has two holes in his stomach. Are they both leaking?" He looked over at Dr. Patel.

She acknowledged, with a nod. "The one is not so much, but the other one is very much so. His skin around the holes is not as red as when he came here, but there is still a lot of leakage," she replied

Dr. O'Conner continued, "He has septic now, and his two PICC lines are infected."

What more is Ray going to be forced to endure? I asked myself. I put my head down and pinched the top of my nose with my fingers. This helps me to not cry. Suddenly, there was a pile of tissues plopped in front of me, and people were asking me if I was all right. What if I wasn't? It wasn't going to change a thing.

I was preparing myself for Dr. O'Conner to say that they were going to take the PICC lines out, and put new ones in, and put Ray on stronger antibiotics, but my prayers from yesterday were answered.

Dr. O'Conner, still having a conversation with only Dr. Patel, asked, "We did cultures didn't we?"

"Yes. The infection is in his blood," she replied.

Nancy had warned me that this is a common happening with these PICC lines when I talked to her last week, after Dr. O'Conner said that Ray had quality of life. She said that people usually get septic or pneumonia and die before the three-month limit is up to have the PICC lines in. With the way that Ray's fighting, I'm not so sure that will happen.

A doctor from the regional NYS DDSO walked in late and sat down near Dr. O'Conner. Dr. O'Conner continued, "There's nothing more that we can do for Ray. There is no one disagreeing with giving Ray comfort care at this point, but Ray has no guardian." I asked, in the general direction of the state workers sitting at the table, how this could be after all of the years that Ray's been a ward of the state. Joe Griffin tried to give an explanation. It sounded to me like some bureaucratic mumbo jumbo that some politician had screwed up. I didn't catch the department that was responsible for Ray's dilemma.

Dr. O'Conner and the doctor who came in late were having an agitated discussion over who could handle giving permission to start Ray's comfort care. What they wanted to do was to wean Ray off of his antibiotics, and to allow the infection to take over his body, and when he was unconscious to take out the artificial nutrition. Is this what they have to resort to so that they can get around the stupid laws in this state?

My sister, Mary, was concerned that when the infection attacked Ray's organs that he would feel pain. I tried reassuring her. "Mary, I watched Mike's dad pass away. He had a fever but felt no pain. It was very peaceful. Mary, they won't let Ray suffer. They are taking good care of him here," I said.

She hadn't been around enough to see how compassionate the workers of Northbrook were. I know that I had some complaints about how things were handled the first few days Ray was at Northbrook, but I also I know that the workers at Northbrook are all feeling the same pain and helplessness that we feel. How could you look at Ray day after day and not be upset at what's happening to him?

The meeting ended with no resolution. Not a big surprise for me. From what I could understand, the doctor who came in late was going to talk to the director of medical services of the regional NYS DDSO, who was also a doctor, and that director of medical services was going to contact Northbrook to tell them if they could carry out Dr. O'Conner's plan for Ray.

After the meeting, Joe Griffin came and sat down next to me. In his freckled hand was a prepared list of attorneys that he knew dealt in guardianship matters. He was the only person from the state who was trying to help my family, and he wasn't the one who created this mess. He never ignored any of my calls, and he gave me straightforward answers if he had them. I always appreciated his efforts, even though I didn't always like his answers.

Together Joe and I scanned the list of attorneys to see if there were any that I recognized. There was a law firm on the list that I dealt with every day in my job. I'd give them a call if we needed to go for guardianship. "Would it help if I had connections in the state government?" I asked Joe.

"Yeah," he replied.

"Well, my district administrator is from a big political family. He's an ex-senator's brother," I said. I made a mental note to talk to him the next time I went into work.

Dr. O'Conner and the doctor who came in late left the room in conversation. Chaplain O'Shay took my family down to his office, and we all held hands and prayed for a swift end to our dilemma. He then gave us communion. "You know, when you have communion, you are closer to Jesus, and when you are closer to Jesus, you are closer to your sister who has passed on. You have all gone through so much," he told us. "God will be with you to strengthen you." He already has. Our angels have all been working overtime.

My family and I went up to Ray's room. He was smiley today and playing with his big zebra. I put in his *Garfield* DVD, and we sat around and talked. Mary sat on Ray's bed because there wasn't any other place to sit. "Hi, Raymond," Mary said, in a little-girl voice. Mary hadn't seen Ray in years. She's the oldest sibling, so she remembers when Ray still lived at home. "His hair is a lot greyer than I remember. What happened to his curls? His hair used to be so curly," she said. She played catch with him for awhile and then just sat watching him.

Ray's nurses—his "girlfriends"—kept coming into the room to check on him. My mom told me that there's an aide who comes in to check on Ray every day before she leaves. She changes him, then sings the song "That's What Friends Are For."

Almost anyone who walks by the room stops in to say hi to Ray or to my family, even the cleaning people. Everyone loves Raymond. They're going to miss his smile, his big, big smile.

The people here are all so joyful and caring. Lynn and I decided that if we have to go into a nursing home we wanted to come to this one. We said that we could have wheelchair races, but by that time our minds would probably be so far gone that we wouldn't even know each other. We'd be looking at each other and wondering, why does she look like me?

It's hard for me to believe that only two weeks have passed since Ray has been in Northbrook. So much has happened. My emotions have been tested and stretched to the limit.

It's after 9:00 PM, and my family hasn't heard anything from Dr. O'Conner or the doctor from the state. Now it'll be the waiting game until Monday.

February 11, Saturday

I had a horrible night's sleep. I didn't take my anti-anxiety medicine last night. I instead took three valerian root capsules to calm me. I thought that I'd get a better sleep that way. Wrong, wrong, wrong. I was listless. Mike and I both kept coughing and disturbing each other's sleep. I must have woken up at least five times.

I'm not going to see Ray today, and I feel so guilty about it. I need to get my house and clothes in order so that I don't feel so overwhelmed on Monday when I start the work week. Thank God that Mike is busy with tax clients and Paul is busy with work and college studies. At least I don't have to feel guilty about ignoring them. Sometimes I cook food for my son so that he doesn't starve, but, really, all I have to be concerned about is Ray and myself.

Something made me check my cell phone today. I had two voice-mail messages. They were from Joe Griffin. I called the phone number Joe left on my voice mail. I knew that it wasn't his work number. I have that memorized. What could be so important that he would call me when he wasn't working, and from his home, yet. His wife answered the phone. I wondered if he told her what was going on with Ray. She went to get Joe. "It doesn't look good, Pat," he said. "I don't think the state is going to go for Dr. O'Conner's plan. I don't think that they'll okay withdrawal of treatment."

I think that Joe had been talking to the director of medical services, or word somehow had gotten to him. I was taken by surprise by his call, so that everything he said didn't register. I asked him, "Can I have this director of medical services—Dr. Monin, is that her name? Can I have her phone number?" I was surprised, but Joe gave it to me. I love that man. He was trying to help as best he could. He had a conscience, and that's why he was bothered by what was happening.

"I think you should start guardianship proceedings," Joe told me.

"Thank you. Thanks for calling me on the weekend," I said.

"Not a problem," he replied. "Do you still have the list of attorneys that I gave you?"

I called my mom and dad. They weren't too keen on going for guardianship, but I told them I'd just call and ask questions. They thought that Ray wouldn't hold on for long and that we'd be wasting our time and money.

I took out the list. First, I called my friend, Ginny, who had a friend, Julie, who worked at the largest law firm on the list, the one who I dealt with on a daily basis. I figured that if I went with a big law firm they could move the proceedings along quicker. Ginny called back and said that she had talked with Julie. Ginny told me, "Julie said to call this phone number and tell them that you want to speak to attorney Jackson. He won't be in the office today, but they will page him, and he'll call you back. Tell him that Julie said to call."

I called the phone number that Ginny gave me, and the woman answering said that they will contact attorney Jackson. I was impressed. I had never heard of attorneys on call on the weekend, except criminal attorneys when people got arrested. About 15 minutes later, he called me. Now I was really impressed

"Julie Henderson told me to call and ask for you," I began.

From the start, Mr. Jackson was all huffy, like, how dare I bother him on the weekend. "We don't have a Julie Henderson working for our firm," he said.

Did he think that I was making this up? "Well, she's been working there for 12 years," I informed him. Then I tried humoring him, with, "Well, it's a large firm." I didn't want to get on his bad side. I really, really needed him to want to help me. My humoring wasn't working, so I continued on. "I have a mentally retarded brother who has been in a group home run by the state since he was little. Now he's gravely ill, and he's being kept alive with artificial nutrition through an IV line. We want to have that withdrawn, but, because he has no guardian, we…"

Mr. Jackson interrupted me with, "What do you mean, he doesn't have a guardian?"

"The state never appointed a guardian for him," I replied.

"He has to have a guardian. How could he not have a guardian? The state has to be his guardian," he said. I'm not stupid. I'm not making up this crap! I wanted to yell into the phone. Why would I make this up and be wasting my time talking to an arrogant attorney on the weekend?

After a few more minutes of talking to him, he finally believed me, but he made me feel like a moron. "Well, I don't handle guardianship cases," he told me. Why did he put me through all of his abuse if he didn't even handle guardianship cases? "I'll give you the name of the attorney at our firm who handles those cases. Call her today, and she'll help you," he said.

His final sentence was the only one not filled with pompousness. I wondered what kind of cases he did handle. I hoped that it wasn't any ones where his clients needed his sympathy, 'cause they weren't gonna get it.

I called the phone number that attorney Jackson had given me. The woman who answered was wonderful to me. She didn't doubt my story at all. She said to call her on Monday, and she would get the proceedings started. "What will the legal fees be?" I asked.

She told me the fee was between $3,000 and $5,000.

I stifled my gasp. "Okay, I'll have to call my parents and run this by them. Is there any way to speed up this procedure?" I asked. She didn't give me any hope that she could accelerate anything. After the experience with the first attorney, and knowing how much their fee was, I wasn't sure if this firm was the right one.

I called Ginny back and left a message on her voice mail to pass along to Julie that attorney Jackson had no idea who she was. I knew if I told Julie that, she would go in on Monday and make him feel as idiotic as he made me feel today. She didn't take crap from anyone.

I called Joe Griffin back, and told him that I had been in contact with someone from an attorney's office. He was surprised that I could talk to someone on the weekend. What can I say? I know people. When I told him the quote the attorney's office gave me, he was flabbergasted. "Wow, I was thinking more along the lines of maybe $500 to $700," he said. It was expensive, but if that's what it takes to end Ray's suffering, I would pay whatever my parents couldn't.

After that, I went about cleaning and cooking with this guardianship thing weighing heavily on my mind. I just didn't feel right about using that firm after how that first attorney treated me. How could you have someone like that on your payroll?

After my cleaning was done, I went to my parents' house. Mike, Lynn, and I wanted to take Mary out to dinner, even though she said that she didn't feel like going out. I pleaded with Mary, "Come on, what good will it do to stay home and brood? Just go with us and get out of the house." I knew that she was upset about Ray, but jeez, she didn't even have to deal with it every day, like Lynn and I did. If Lynn and I wanted to get out and have a drink, why couldn't Mary humor us and come, too? Finally, with more prodding, she relented.

We went to a Mexican restaurant. Mike was our chauffeur for the night, so Mary and Lynn could have as many beers as they wanted. I had to limit my drinks because alcohol aggravates my irregular heartbeat, which is almost continual lately. After dinner and a couple of beers, we headed home.

On the way, we stopped at a party store for Mike and me to get beads to wear to a Fat Tuesday party that a friend of ours was hosting. Mary bought a soft, furry pink dog for us to give Ray the next time we saw him. That was our big night out. It wasn't very exciting, but it felt good to not be in a hospital or at home playing catch-up on my housework.

February 12, Sunday

I woke up with the same feeling of unease about that law firm. I needed to have someone who cared about me working for me. If they care, they're more willing to fight for you. I just couldn't use that firm. When I went to church, I saw Maria, the wife of our attorney friend, in the pew in front of us. I really felt badly that he wasn't the first attorney whom I asked to help us. I should have listened to Mike. I honestly felt that a larger firm could have helped us faster. Well, I was wrong. I've been wrong a lot these days.

After Mass, a lot of the parishioners stand outside and talk. Maria was there amongst them. "Maria, I need Matt's help," I said. I started telling her about Raymond, and I broke down crying.

"Matt's in the school cafeteria, flipping pancakes. You go talk to him. He'll be able to help," she said. Matt was running a pancake breakfast to benefit the school affiliated with my parish. That was how Mike and I met him, through the multitude of fundraisers for the school, when Paul had attended there. By the time I trotted down the steps to the cafeteria of the school, I had myself composed enough to not blubber after each sentence.

Matt knew the laws pertaining to obtaining guardianship, and within a matter of minutes had a plan all worked out. Screw that big law firm with the pompous ass of an attorney! On Monday, I'm going to call that woman attorney and tell her that we decided not to go for guardianship. I don't like lying, but it wouldn't be a total lie. I'd just be leaving off the "with them" part of my message when I tell her we wouldn't be pursuing guardianship.

Mike went with me to Northbrook today. As soon as I saw Ray, I knew that it wasn't good. He was sleeping, but with his mouth open and slack, to one side. Mike's father looked like that in his final days. Ray's eyes didn't close all the way, and they rolled back into his head, as if he was in some kind of drug-induced coma or something.

When he did awaken, he had a dazed look on his face. He wasn't focusing on anything. Most of the time he looked terrified, and all that he wanted to do was to hold someone's hand. When he was awake, I stroked his hand and talked soothingly to him, then he would pass out again.

Ray's nurse said that he had quite a bit of vomiting. At first it was clear, and then later it turned to a dark brown. While I was there, he threw up dark brown liquid twice, a lot of it. After I wiped Ray up with the towel by his head, I looked into Ray's dresser and found more towels. When they were saturated, I went out into the hallway and nabbed more towels off of the laundry cart.

I told the nurse every time that Ray puked. She told me that she was going to give him something else for his vomiting. I asked the nurse why his vomit would be brown. "It could be from internal bleeding or a bowel obstruction," she replied.

Poor Ray. "How much more can happen to you?" I asked him, as he passed out once more.

A different nurse came in a while later. "Ray has a bowel obstruction that needs to be treated," she said. "I looked at his chart, and it says that he should only be taken to Michael Fitzsimmons Hospital. Is there a reason for that?" she asked. I told her that we weren't happy with the treatment that he was getting at West End. "I see," she said. "Generally, it's because of a certain doctor."

I wanted to say that we don't even know the names of the doctors who treated Ray because we never got to talk to them, but I had more pressing problems at the time.

"What are they going to do to him in the hospital?" I questioned the nurse.

"Well, he has an obstruction. They're going to take care of it and do surgery, if necessary," she replied.

"When will you be taking him? Tomorrow?" I asked.

"No, today," she said.

"Don't you need my parent's permission?" I asked her. They asked their permission for everything else. They always had to sign a consent form.

"No. This is an emergency," she replied.

Okay, no more pussy-footing around. If I was going to save Ray from any more torture, I had to lay it all out on the line for this nurse, whom I had never seen before.

I told her, "Well, on Monday, we're hoping to get permission from someone from the state to stop treatment on Ray."

"Oh, oh," she said, "Had I known, I wouldn't have stuck my foot into this to get this thing going. I was wondering why this poor man's family would be trying further treatment to keep him going. Well, let me see what I can do."

If that's what she thought, why didn't she discuss it with the doctor and my family before she went and tried to have him sent to the hospital? Thank God I was there.

A few minutes later, that nurse came into the room to get me. "Can you come to the nurses' station and talk to Dr. Ernst on the phone?" she asked. Sure, I'd talk to anyone on earth to stop any surgery that was only going to prolong or worsen Ray's suffering.

I explained the guardianship issue and from whom we were waiting for an answer. The family doesn't want Ray to have any further treatment. Why can't the world accept that and grant our wishes?

"Okay, we'll keep Ray there and not treat the bowel obstruction," Dr. Ernst said.

"Can you do that legally?" I asked.

"Yes, we're not withdrawing treatment. We're just not initiating it. Is there a do-not-resuscitate order in Ray's chart?" Dr. Ernst asked.

I thought my parents said that there was. I asked the nurses to check. "Yes, yes, it's in his chart," I was told.

"Good. Well, we'll just leave things as they are. I'll let Dr. O'Conner know our decision," said the doctor.

The nurse apologized for the mix-up. That would have been a major mistake if I hadn't been there to stop it. Thank God that Ray had family checking up on him. I pity the poor people who are incapacitated and have no one looking out for them. I didn't want to imagine what could be happening to them.

The nurse came in later to tell us that Ray would be getting a different anti-nausea medicine and a pain patch. He was already getting pain medicine by subcutaneous injection, but it didn't seem to be enough. If I had two holes in my stomach leaking acid, a fissure inside my abdomen, and a bowel obstruction, I'd need more than just two pain medicines.

A little while later, Lynn came in to relieve Mike and me. While I was filling her in on what had happened earlier, a different nurse came into the room to say that Ray was being taken for a CAT scan because his x-rays showed that he had a bowel obstruction. No kidding, but why was he having a CAT scan when I had just talked to his doctor and we had agreed on no further treatment? I looked at Lynn in astonishment, then back at the nurse.

"When were these x-rays taken?" I asked.

"This morning. Now the next step is for Ray to have a CAT scan done," the nurse replied.

"Where will that be done?" I asked.

The nurse looked at me like I was the dumbest person on earth. "Well, we have to take him out of here," she said.

"Wait a minute. Wait a minute," I said. "We were just told that Ray was going to stay here and that the obstruction wouldn't be treated. I just talked to Dr. Ernst about this."

"Well, I just talked to Dr. O'Conner and he ordered the CAT scan," she replied. Wow, this place was getting as scary as West End Hospital.

"I was told that Dr. O'Conner will know about Dr. Ernst's decision," I said.

"Well, I don't know if I can legally not follow through on this," she said. "Okay, I'll be back."

I paced back and forth. Legally? What is this? She's just supposed to follow a doctor's orders. Is she supposed to be questioning the legality of those orders? And, as for Dr. O'Conner, has he lost his mind? I don't think that he remembers who Ray is. Just two days ago, he was at the meeting to talk about Ray. He wanted to withdraw him from antibiotics and let him pass away. If he remembered that meeting, why would he order Raymond to be taken to West End for tests?

A different nurse came into Ray's room. "Dr. O'Conner said that Ray is to stay here and that we're doing nothing but treating his symptoms," she said.

Well, yeah, is what I wanted to say. But pointing out how stupid the staff was being today wasn't going to help. "Thank you," was all that I said, as I bit my tongue once more and tapped my foot on the floor.

During the week when the regulars were on duty was great, but on weekends when there are all different kinds of people, it's a whole different ball game. Lynn and I decided that we needed to have someone by Ray's side as much as possible on the weekends when the normal staff isn't around. And I'm going to talk to Nancy on Monday to tell her how concerned we are about what happened today.

I called my parents to tell them how bad Ray was. Dad said that he and Mom were coming down to see Ray. "Does it seem like he's near the end?" Dad asked me. I didn't know. I asked the nurse in the room at the time, and she said that she couldn't make that determination.

"We'll be right down," Dad said.

Lynn, Mike, and I planned out our evening. Lynn would stay till Mom and Dad arrived. Mike and I would go to his sister, Ann's, house for dinner. Then I would go home to pack an overnight bag. Then I would go back to Northbrook alone to relieve Mom and Dad and stay the night. If Ray was still bad, Lynn would spend the next night with him.

I went with Mike to Anne's house for a family dinner. Once seated for dinner, we said grace. Today I added a prayer that God would take care of Ray. I was so sure the end was near. I wound up bawling before I finished the words. "Sorry," I said. I didn't want to depress everyone any more than they already were.

I ate and packed up plates for Paul and my parents, then went home to pack up my overnight bag—a book, water, snacks, phone charger, laptop computer, paper, pen, slippers, and a flashlight.

I got to Northbrook after visiting hours were over. As previously arranged, I called the security desk and told them I was given permission by Charmaine, the floor nurse, to stay the night. She told me that security would watch me on their cameras for my safety as I made my way to the front doors.

When I got into the building, the security man showed me the cameras that had followed me as I walked up the long driveway. There was my van on the monitor. The cameras were on 24 hours a day and there was always someone at the desk watching them. The rumors that my sister heard about how unsafe Northbrook was were wrong.

Everyone in this facility takes great pride in their work. The security guard told me, "Tell Charmaine I took care of you." I'd make sure she got the message. I wanted to make that man happy so that he'd be making my safety a priority.

Poor Ray is so uncomfortable. He keeps waking up and gagging or raising his arm as if to grab at something. He growls so much, and I don't think I can take his suffering all night. The aides brought in a reclining chair and a warm, fluffy blanket for me to use while I stayed by Ray's side.

He finally fell asleep for awhile. I hope that it lasts a long, long time, I thought, before I turned off the light in Ray's room about 10:00 PM. I'm going to try to get some sleep, but I think that it's a futile effort. If Ray's not gagging or crying, the staff is wandering the halls. They don't talk in whispers around here. I shut the door, and it was a bit more quiet.

February 13, Monday

Ray-Ray was so bad last night that I thought his days were numbered. All night long he woke up and looked lost and afraid. I spent the entire night in the reclining chair by his bed. He'd wake up and let out a high-pitched cry. Oh, it hurt my ears. Then he'd flail around in bed. I had to keep grabbing his hands, calling his name, and talking to him in a soothing voice to calm him down. Then he'd sleep for about 15 minutes or more. I would doze off. Then he'd wake up, and it would start all over again.

A couple of times in the night, the nurses came in to change Ray and give him his meds. Other than that, it was just me and Ray in that cold, dark room. Finally, daylight chased the cruel night away. What a long, grueling night it had been. I must have gotten some sleep because I didn't feel as exhausted as I thought I would be, or maybe my adrenalin is in overdrive from all of the stress.

Mom and Dad came in a little early today, about 8:30 AM, to relieve me. Chaplain O'Shay came in a little while after that. Mom told me a few days ago that he comes up every day he's at this facility to see Ray. He told Mom, "Every time I see a zebra, I'll think of Ray." That big floppy zebra is always by Ray's side.

I sat on the mat on the floor between Ray's bed and the wall. The staff puts that on the floor when Ray's active in case he falls out of bed. Still resting on the mat, I called my boss to tell her about Ray. I wasn't going into work today after being awake most of last night. I called the woman attorney I had spoken to on Saturday, and left a message on her voice mail telling her that we didn't need her services because Ray had taken a turn for the worse. Well, I wasn't lying. Ray was so bad. He can't last much longer.

Dr. Patel came in at 9:00 AM and talked to us about Ray, after examining him. He has the beginnings of pneumonia, which she opted not to treat with more antibiotics. She explained that the medicine in the form of a patch on his arm won't kick in for two days. She put him temporarily on something else to make Ray feel "more comfortable," as she put it. He didn't have that look of abject misery on his face this morning, but he still wasn't focusing on anything.

I came home, took a bath, and lit incense. I felt so contaminated from Ray coughing on me all night, and there was a smell that I can't explain. It wasn't poop or vomit. It wasn't decay. It just didn't smell clean. It was the smell of death. I've smelled it before coming from people I know who have died from cancer shortly after my seeing them. I couldn't get the smell out of my nose. I had to stop thinking about it. It grossed me out.

I plopped down on my wonderful, fluffy bed and passed out for hours. When I woke up, I called Matt, our friend, the attorney. I left a message on his voice mail telling him that we wouldn't be needing him because Ray had taken a turn for the worse.

I called Ray's room, and my mom said that his breathing was horrible. She put the phone up to Ray, but I couldn't hear anything. She also said that the doctor said that Ray wouldn't last much longer.

I was in a quandary. Should I stay overnight with Lynn? Should I go to Northbrook for a few hours, then come home and get a good night's sleep, because tomorrow would be my turn to stay with Ray overnight? My brain is tired, and I don't want to make decisions anymore. I just want someone to take over for a little while.

I called the nurses' station and asked to speak to Nancy. I told her that I was concerned about the nurses wanting to take Ray away—not once, but twice—for treatment yesterday. Her answer to my concern didn't quell my anxiety. Nancy said, "Well, they would have looked at Ray's chart after deciding to do more tests and would have seen that no new procedures are to be done on him." Aren't they supposed to look at the chart *before* they decide on treatment, not after? My brain hurt too much to argue with her.

After I hung up the phone, I wondered how many patients are in health care facilities and don't have anyone constantly by their side looking out for them. I felt sorry for every last one of those people, knowing from experience what could happen to them.

I called Lynn and told her to call me when she got to the hospital. I don't always get the whole picture from my parents. Lynn called from Ray's room, and said he looked much better than he did yesterday. It must be the new drugs that he's getting.

Lynn convinced me not to come down. She sent Mom and Dad home, too, because the weather was pretty bad, with snow and whiteouts. She said that I could call her before I went to bed to get an update. If Ray got worse, she would call me.

My mom called when she got home, around 4:30 PM, and said that Ray looked much better. He pooped. After that, he improved. "Do you think that he was vomiting up all that stuff just because he didn't poop?" I asked her. I found that totally mind-boggling.

"I don't know. He was like that once, before, and they put a tube down his throat," she replied. That didn't answer my question, but, hey, Ray was better. It must have been the poop backed up in his system. Pooping is a good thing. I'll have to make sure that I do it more often.

"Mom, no one has said anything about the state's decision, have they?" I asked.

"No," she replied.

Someone was supposed to contact us on Friday, and now another work day has gone by without anyone calling us. "I can't believe that no one has the courtesy to call us to tell us what's going on," I said to her.

We waited all day for a call from Dr. Monin, the director of medical services for the regional NYS DDSO, or Dr. O'Conner to tell us if Dr. O'Conner's plan put forth at the meeting was going to be acceptable to the state. No one called. No one had answers for us? Maybe these people are compassionate with their patients; but what about the families of the patients? Don't they think about them? It's not like we were asking for Ray to have a lollipop or something insignificant like that. Ray was dying, and we wanted to end his suffering. Dogs are treated more humanely than my brother is.

I'm getting angry again, and now I have chest pains. I took a tranquilizer and went back to bed.

February 15, Wednesday

I don't know what keeps me going. My emotions are running the gamut—anger, then sorrow, then helplessness, then anger, then confusion, then anguish. They change like the weather, from the time I get up, until the time I go to bed. I fear that I might go over the brink into insanity. I can't be of any use to Ray if I'm in jail or some mental institution, so I have to try to control my emotions. There's no end in sight to this nightmare that my family is in.

The first thing I did when I got to work today was to talk to my district administrator. He was related to a large family involved in politics in New York State. I wanted to ask if he could be of any help. He listened attentively to my story about Ray, and took down people's names and phone numbers. I broke down, crying, at one point. He waited patiently until I had composed myself. Then he asked, "Now, what do you want me to do?"

I thought I'd start with a small request. "I want an answer from Dr. Monin, a yes-or-no answer. Will they allow Raymond to be withdrawn from antibiotics as discussed on Friday or, no, they won't allow it? That's all. Just yes or no," I replied.

"Is she in? Has she been on vacation?" he asked.

"I doubt if she's on vacation," I said. "I know that someone from the NYS DDSO was in contact with her on Friday. She said that she was going to talk to legal counsel, and we would have an answer as to whether Dr. O'Conner's plan was approved or not. It's Wednesday, and my family has had no word. We were told that people from Northbrook hadn't heard anything yet, either."

"I'll talk to my nephew. He's a state assemblyman. Pat, if you need anything, just ask. All I can do is say 'yes' or 'no,'" he finished.

So many people are willing to help, but their hands are tied by the screwed-up state laws.

When I got back to my desk, I decided to call Dr. Monin myself to see if she had been in her office. Her secretary answered the phone.

"Can you tell me if Dr. Monin has been in her office?" I inquired.

"Yes. Why?" she asked.

"I'm the sister of Raymond — — —," I said. "I'm sure that Dr. Monin knows of his case. I want to know why she hasn't given an answer to anyone."

"I don't understand what you're talking about. An answer to what?" the secretary asked.

"An answer as to whether Raymond's doctor can withdraw antibiotics or not," I replied.

The secretary acted like she had no idea what I was talking about. "You say that people have called. What people are you talking about?" she asked. Now she was being evasive.

"Well, Joe Griffin for one," I replied.

"He didn't call," she said.

"He e-mailed Dr. Monin yesterday and said that he was waiting for an answer by the end of the day," I said.

"Well, here is his e-mail," she said. "He isn't asking for anything. He's just giving an update on Ray's condition."

She knew very well what I was talking about. I didn't have patience for playing games. "I'd like a call back from Dr. Monin," I said.

"Well, she isn't in, but I will give her your message," she said. First she was in, then she wasn't, when I wanted to talk to her.

I tried doing my job, and I did get a little done, but again my mind was elsewhere. I called my mom at the hospital in Ray's room. Ray was being taken to West End for another new PICC line to be put in, because the current one had clogged. Again my parents were being made to go to West End to sign a consent form.

"Mom, don't sign it," I pleaded.

"Pat, I'm too tired to argue," she said.

So, Ray was going off to get a new PICC line put in. Northbrook was haggling with the New York State Medicaid Department because they didn't want to pay for an ambulance to send Ray to the hospital. I can't believe it. They willingly pay for endless days in the hospital to keep him alive and continue his suffering because they won't allow him to be taken off of life-sustaining treatment, but they won't pay for an ambulance so that he can go to get the treatment they mandated.

Last week, when Ray had his PICC line replaced, they made an aide from his group home drive an hour to go pick Ray up and put him in his wheelchair. Then the aide dragged Ray's IV pole behind him while he was taking Ray to the wheelchair van. A nurse from Northbrook had to accompany Ray to make sure that none of his IV lines were pulled out. The aide then had to wait at West End until the PICC line was in. Then he brought Ray back to Northbrook. This is how our wonderful, caring state takes such good care of its wards.

At lunchtime, the elusive Dr. Monin called me back. She said, "I don't understand what you're talking about. I talked to Dr. O'Conner on Friday. I told him to start comfort care."

"What do you mean?" I asked. I don't think that she understood what comfort care means. It means taking someone off of everything and making them comfortable while they pass through the final stage of their life. The state wouldn't let us do that. "We were told that everything was to stay as it was until someone heard from you," I said.

"Well, I talked to Dr. O'Conner," she said.

"Now, I understand that Ray's nourishment can't be withdrawn," I said, "but, at the meeting, Dr. O'Conner was talking about withdrawing Ray's antibiotics."

"Ray's septic is getting better," Dr. Monin said. "Does he have a fever?" she asked.

"He's had a fever all along," I replied. What was she talking about? Ray's septic was getting better?

"Have you ever thought about Hospice?" she asked. Why was she bringing that up? We were told that we were not allowed to think about it.

"Yes," I replied, "and we were told that we couldn't do it because they won't allow anyone to have an IV."

If she knew what she was talking about, if she checked into what Hospice did, herself, she wouldn't have asked me that question. Anyway, if we were allowed to go through Hospice for end-of-life care, why wasn't the state setting up Hospice or comfort care? Why was it up to my family? Why wasn't anyone from the state helping us?

"I told Joe Griffin to advise your family to go for guardianship," Dr. Monin went on.

Wait a minute. If Dr. Monin had talked to Dr. O'Conner on Friday and told him that he could start comfort care, like she said she did, why would my family have to go for guardianship?

Dr. Monin was spinning around in circles. Was she trying to confuse the issue, or was she really this confused, herself?

"We were told that would be a lengthy and expensive process," I said.

"Well, I know that there are attorneys at West End who can do it pretty quickly," she said. I wanted to tell her that I wouldn't step inside that place again unless I was unconscious and there was no one to tell them not to take me there. Ray's time there was so chaotic; God only knows what the attorneys from that place would do.

I didn't have all day to ramble on about Ray's inadequate care and how the state had screwed up. I cut the conversation short. "Okay, so, all along, Dr. O'Conner has been the one not communicating with us," I said.

"Well, I can tell you that I talked to him on Friday," Dr. Monin stated.

"Well, thank you very much for calling me back," I finished.

I was fuming. I was pacing back and forth. My co-workers were watching me, wondering what I was going to do next. I finally sat down at my desk and pulled out my list of phone numbers from Northbrook. I've taken to carrying folders with lists and forms and information on Ray everywhere I go. You never know when they will come in handy.

I called the director of Northbrook again. When she answered the phone, I inquired, "Do you have authority over Dr. O'Conner?"

She chuckled. "Yes, I guess I do," she replied.

"You know," I said, "we had a meeting on Friday about my brother Raymond and were waiting for an answer as to whether we could take Raymond off of his antibiotics. I just had a conversation with Dr. Monin, the director of medical services of the regional WNY DDSO, and she says that she talked to Dr. O'Conner on Friday. You know what? Can I come and talk to you?"

"Of course you can," she replied. She was so accommodating, even though she was probably thinking, what does that pushy woman want now?

I called Lynn to tell her that there was something fishy going on, and I didn't know who was telling the truth, but I was going to talk to the director of Northbrook. I would meet Lynn at Northbrook when she came to see Ray at her usual time.

Within 15 minutes, I was at Northbrook, sitting across the desk from Norma Jean Smythe once again.

She informed me, "Dr. Monin has not called Northbrook or spoken to Dr. O'Conner. We haven't received any directives from the state."

She called Nancy to come down to corroborate her story. After that, I felt really stupid. Now I didn't know who to believe.

Norma Jean then called Dr. O'Conner and asked him if he had heard from Dr. Monin. He had heard from her. If he did, why didn't anyone notify our family? Things were happening so fast that I wasn't able to ask that question. I was trying to listen in on Norma Jean's one-sided conversation with Dr. O'Connor.

From what I gathered Dr. Monin hadn't said to start comfort care. She hadn't said to consider Hospice, but she gave the okay to not start any new treatments. Dr. Monin had misled me into thinking that Dr. O'Connor was holding up Ray's comfort care when nothing had changed. Not starting new treatment—how is that going to help Ray?

While Raymond's treatment was being discussed, a light must have gone on in Dr. O'Conner's head. Why was Ray having a new PICC line put in?

Norma Jean called the hospital and tracked down where Ray was. He had been at the hospital for hours, but the procedure to put his PICC line in hadn't yet begun. I think that was the only time in my life that I was thankful a medical procedure was being held up for hours. Norma Jean called Dr. O'Conner back to tell him the news.

As he called the hospital to cancel the procedure, I crossed my fingers, put them to my lips, and said, "Let's all pray that this works." The angels were on our side today. Ray was going to be brought back to Northbrook without a new PICC line. One small victory for our side.

I didn't know if I should tell anyone else besides my family what just took place, but I had a feeling I shouldn't. Why did I have to be so secretive? We hadn't gone against what Dr. Monin had said.

"Your parents are going to be so confused," Nancy said to me, and she left the room.

All I could picture was Mom and Dad waiting for Ray to have his procedure done, and then being told that it wasn't going to happen, and getting mad at the staff of West End for screwing up, yet again.

I got up from my chair and went around to where Norma Jean stood. "Thank you so much. Can I give you a hug?" I asked her. I always ask first with people whom I don't know. Some people don't like to be touched. "I'm so sorry that I came in here all mad," I said.

"That's okay," Norma Jean told me. She shook her head in disbelief. "Your family is going through so much."

I went to the lobby and patiently waited for my parents to walk through the doors. An hour went by, and still no parents. In the meantime, I called Lynn and told her to come directly to me, and don't ask anyone any questions.

I gave up waiting for my parents and went up to Ray's floor to see if he had come back, because I knew that he would have come through a different entrance. As soon as I got up to Ray's floor, he was being wheeled down the hall by the ambulance drivers. Ray was smiling away like he had been on some great adventure. He had a hold of a pretty blonde ambulance attendant's hand, and was gazing up at her, all gaga-eyed. After the attendants put Ray back in his bed, the pretty blonde said, "Raymond you can let go of my hand, now." He kept holding on, and laughed a dirty old man's laugh. He just loved the pretty ladies, especially blondes. What a silly little man he was.

Minutes after the aides got Ray situated in his bed, Lynn came walking down the hall. I initiated the conversation because I didn't want her to start asking questions. "I'm still waiting for Mom and Dad. I don't understand why they aren't here yet," I said.

Lynn informed me, "The hospital told them to go home. It wasn't necessary for them to wait. It would be a long time until they took Ray."

Well, that worked out better. At least they wouldn't be there wondering what was going on, but now they didn't have a clue what happened, and I'd have to tell them.

There were too many people coming and going in Ray's room for me to have a private conversation with Lynn, so we took the sandwiches that she had picked up for dinner for us, and went down to the cafeteria to talk. It was 4:00 PM, and absolutely no one was there except a man setting the tables for the evening meal.

I filled Lynn in on what had happened. "I'm so glad that you're such a fighter," she told me.

"Lynn, I don't want to be," I said. "What's happening to Ray is wrong, just wrong. When he's gone, we have to do something so that this never, never, never happens to anyone again. I just don't know what that should be yet. I'll figure it out. I will."

During our whole conversation, a little old man kept walking into the dining room, looking toward us, and then turning away and leaving. He did this a few times. Finally, he shuffled up to our table, and said, "I usually sit there," and continued to stand by us.

"That's okay. We're done. We're leaving," Lynn told him.

"No, that's all right. I'll come back," he said dejectedly.

"No, no, we really are done," Lynn insisted again. We picked up our garbage and got up.

The little old man's shoulders slouched even more as he stood by the table, looking confused. "Now I don't have a place setting," he said. Our table hadn't been set because we had been sitting there.

I felt badly for the man. I said to Lynn, "That must be one of their Alzheimer's patients. The poor guy, we must have upset his routine."

Lynn said, "Don't laugh, that may be us in a few years."

"What do you mean? That's me now," I said to Lynn.

We looked at each other and laughed all the way up the elevator to Ray's room. Thank God that I have her to get through this hell with.

I called Dad from Ray's phone. Suddenly, I felt like I was in the middle of some espionage story. I whispered into the phone, "Dad, I'm coming over to talk to you, but I can't say what it is over the phone. This one might be bugged."

"What?" he asked. I had him totally confused.

"I have to come and talk to you about something. I can't tell you about it here. There are too many ears," I said. I could have some fun for a little while and pretend I was a spy couldn't I?

On the day that I was supposed to get a break from this whole mess with Ray, I again was going over to my parents' house to have a talk. What a God-awful long day this has been. Will I ever be able to just get up, go to work, and come home to do whatever I want in peace?

February 16, Thursday

Today Dr. Monin called me at work, fishing for answers. I was taken aback because the entire time that Ray has been suffering, no one from the NYS DDSO has initiated a phone call to my family except for the workers from the group home and Joe Griffin. I was still upset because Dr. Monin made me look stupid in front of Norma Jean and Nancy, two people whom I've come to admire.

I said, "Dr. Monin, I'm not talking to you anymore. You misled me into believing that Dr. O'Conner had all of the control over Raymond. New York State with its laws has all the power. *You* have the power, and I suggest that you call Northbrook if you want to find out anything."

She was all defensive. "I called Dr. O'Conner on Friday and told him to start comfort care," she said.

She must have had a completely different idea of what comfort care meant than what it really was. She had to have known that the state wouldn't allow comfort care. Or was she really that confused? Anyway, she wasn't the least bit put off by my remark.

Dr. Monin pressed on. "Did Ray go to West End yesterday?" she asked.

Stupid me answered, "Yes."

"Did he come back?" she asked.

Why was she asking me? She must have had that information. If she didn't, she should have been able to get it. But dumb me still was answering her prying questions.

"Yes," I replied.

"Did he get a PICC line in?" she asked.

Okay, that was enough of her snooping. I answered, "I'm not talking to you anymore. You need to talk to Northbrook if you want any answers. I'm not talking to you anymore." I hung up on her while she was trying to tell me some more malarkey. Oh, that felt good.

I left a message with Norma Jean and Nancy, asking them to call me back. I wanted them to know that Dr. Monin had called trying to get information on Ray. Then I called Dad in Ray's room to tell him what had just happened, in case Dr. Monin tried calling him. I doubted that she would. If she was the least bit interested in Ray, she would have shown her face or talked to anyone involved with Ray long before this.

After I got on the elevator to go up to Ray's floor, a man in his wheelchair, looking in his thirties, was trying to back his wheelchair into the elevator. I wanted to help him, but he had such a look of determination in his eyes that I just pushed the button to keep the elevator door open instead of helping him. His face was slack on one side like he may have had a stroke. I asked him questions that he didn't answer. He just kept his gaze on his lap. When the elevator doors opened on his floor, he made a quick exit. A whiff of the air told me that he had wet himself. That must have been a degrading experience for such a young man.

I saw that Nancy wasn't at the nurses' station while on my way to Ray's room. I'll probably talk to her tomorrow. Ray's favorite nurse, Laura, was on duty tonight. His eyes light up when he hears her voice. She comes in to sit with him on her breaks if one of us isn't there. Ray just tugs at everyone's hearts.

She came in tonight to give Ray his shot. She pulled back the sheet and looked for the meatiest part of his body, but there wasn't one. She settled on his thigh. He cried out in pain when the needle went in. Laura rubbed the spot. She said, "I feel so bad. The poor thing; he has no meat left. I just hate sticking him anymore. He cries every time." What are we gonna do with poor Ray? It's even getting hard to give him his pain meds now.

Later, Laura came in while Ray and I were watching *The Sound of Music*. "Oh, that's my favorite musical," she said. She started singing along with the video. Ray smiled away. "The rest of the crew doesn't like my singing, but you do, don't you, Ray?" she asked him. She walked down the hall, singing, "Doe, a deer, a female deer, ray, a drop of golden sun…" It's so nice to hear singing instead of that lady across the hall who keeps yelling, "Nurse! Nurse! Can someone help me?"

Tonight, when I was waiting in the hall while the aides were changing Ray, that same woman called me over to her room. "Can you tell me where I am?" she asked me.

"You're at Northbrook Nursing Home," I answered. The poor thing doesn't remember that she's been here for weeks. She probably doesn't remember that she calls the nurse every five minutes, either. I have to remember that when her beckoning annoys me.

I went back into Ray's room, held his hand, and wiped my tears away with the other hand. We finished watching *The Sound of Music*. This is the first time in my life that I've seen it from beginning to end.

February 17, Friday

It was Lynn's turn to see Ray today.

I got calls back from Norma Jean and Nancy. Each of them chuckled when I told them of my conversation with Dr. Monin and how I had hung up on her. There's no love lost between the workers of Northbrook and the employees of New York State.

After talking to Norma Jean and Nancy, I was calmed down and actually was getting some of my work done. Then Dad called. "We're going for guardianship. Can you call Matt [our friend, the lawyer]?" he asked.

I started talking to myself. "Why me? Why me? Why do I always have to initiate everything? Because I'm a big mouth. That's why," I said to myself. My co-workers are getting used to my babbling to myself.

Okay, now to make more phone calls. "Hi, Matt, my family decided to go for guardianship of my brother, after all. We thought Ray would die this past weekend, but he's such a fighter that he came through."

He probably thought I was a ditz, vacillating the way that I was about proceeding with guardianship for Ray. My life has been vacillating for so long that it seems normal for me to be in constant turmoil.

Matt said, "Well, I'll be glad to help you, but I'm leaving for vacation for a week, starting tomorrow." Nothing has been easy these past few months. Why would this be? "I'll get the paperwork ready for you to pick up on Tuesday," he continued. "You know, Monday is a holiday. Oh, wait, why don't I drop it off at your house today, and you can get your parents to fill out their forms? Your siblings can get their forms signed, too. I'll tell you which ones to bring to the office on Tuesday to be typed and, hopefully, by the time I get back, your siblings will have sent back their forms."

Well, there went my spare time. I'm complaining; but I really don't mind any time spent helping Ray. I'd move heaven and earth for him.

Matt dropped off the forms with explanations on all of them. After dinner, Mike and I went to Mom's and Dad's once more to fill out paperwork.

Then we went home again to get together the forms for the out-of-town siblings. They had to fill them out, get them notarized, and send the originals back, hopefully by the end of next week.

Lynn called tonight to give me an update on Ray. He's getting sublingual morphine now. They stopped giving him his pain shots because there is so little meat on Ray that even the subcutaneous injections would hit bone. He cried out in pain every time the nurses gave him an injection. He was supposed to get them six times a day. I wish that Dr. Monin could come in and see the condition that Ray is in. How can the state be so insensitive and cruel to such a sweet, innocent person?

February 18, Saturday

Today my head is spinning. I'm trying to figure out the logistics of getting all of the consent forms to my siblings—one in Massachusetts, one in Pennsylvania, and one in Georgia. We'll have to fax or send the forms by mail. I had Mike fax the form with a sample to my one brother at work.

Then I called my other brother from Massachusetts to ask him if there was a way to fax the form to him. He had a fax with his home phone. He needed to switch his phone to the fax. All I had to do was put the form in my fax, dial his home phone number, press the "send" button, and, voilà, it should work. Mike tried once, twice; it wasn't going through.

My brother from Massachusetts called me back. "I'm going to have to work on it. It should be working. I don't know why it isn't. You know, Pat, I told Mike to take care of you," he said.

"Mike is in the middle of tax season. He's doing the best he can. He cleans and shops when he has time," I said.

"Well, you need some down time," he said.

"I know that," I said, "but I'm here, and every time I think that I'm going to have a day off, something happens, and there I am in the midst of it, trying to take care of it."

"Well, you need to relax," he said.

"I try. I really try. It's just that I'm here, and there is no way of getting away from this nightmare," I said.

Even if I could get out of town, I couldn't do that to Ray. I have to stay the course until this is over, even though it might kill me. Now I'm being melodramatic. I'm going to be fine, I think.

I called Mary on Mike's cell phone and, miraculously, she also had a fax with her home phone. I faxed the form to her along with a sample of the one I had filled out so that she could see which boxes to mark off and the order of the appointed guardians. We wanted everyone's forms to be exact.

My brother from Massachusetts called me back about half an hour later. "Try faxing that form to me now. I changed the cable to my phone," he said.

Down to the basement I went once more to interrupt Mike and his tax client to try the fax. It went through. I got a call a few minutes later from my brother in Massachusetts. The sample form that I faxed him was all squiggled up, so I pulled mine out and talked him through filling his out.

Phew. I could finally relax. All of my siblings had their forms. My job was done for the moment. Why is the state making it so difficult for my family when they were the ones who didn't appoint a guardian for Ray? Why couldn't they help us with all of this crap? Why have they abandoned Ray? I don't think I will ever get an answer to those questions.

I took a valerian root and tried to relax. By now it was 12:00 noon. I was getting sleepy, so I took a much-deserved nap. I woke up and played a few hands of my new obsession—spider solitaire.

The phone rang. It was Mary. She told me, "Jill [Mary's mother-in-law] was talking, and she thinks that if we go for guardianship we'll get saddled with all the medical bills."

"Mary, we already went through that. I asked our attorney, and he said no," I informed her.

I had to reassure her that we had everything under control, that our attorney handled other guardianship cases and knew what he was doing. After I hung up from her, I took a tranquilizer to calm down. I can't take the stress anymore.

I went to see Ray tonight. I was waiting for Mike to get done with his clients, but it was 5:45 PM, and he still wasn't finished. I had to go alone. I parked on the street, a place I knew was well lit and within site of the front doors of Northbrook, where I would be safe.

Ray was sleeping when I got to his room, and was facing the wall. As soon as he heard me taking off my coat and hanging it up, his eyes popped open. He had that scared and lonely look in his eyes. I sat down beside him, patted his hand, and he grabbed mine. He seemed uncomfortable. He kept trying to move like he wanted to sit up. I knew he couldn't do that, so I kept trying to get him to relax. He'd close his eyes for a few minutes, then open them, and try to move again. He would not let go of my hand, not for anything. So, I just sat there until he dozed off, gently removed my hand, and went about what I had to do.

The top drawer in Ray's dresser has become our snack drawer. Between Mom, Dad, Lynn, and me, we keep it stocked. We never know when we'll have to stay longer than planned. We take each day as it comes. Sometimes Ray's okay, sometimes he's dreadful.

As Lynn and I had discussed, I put the guardianship papers for her to fill out in that same drawer, under the snack bars. Then Ray woke up with that sad, scared look again. I sat down and held his hand again, and he fell asleep.

I found out today that Ray's nurse, Laura, has a baby herself, so she can identify with Ray and his mentality. She told me that she had given Ray his morphine just after my parents left. "He had that scared look in his eyes again," she said.

I always breathe a sigh of relief when Laura's on duty. I know that Ray will get extra-special care when she works. She looks in on him each time she passes his room.

The workers here at Northbrook are all getting familiar with my family because they see us so much. The one aide reminds me of Alice, the housekeeper on *The Brady Bunch*. She comes in to sit with Ray when he's alone and she has a break from her busy schedule. I don't think that anyone else in this place gets as many visitors as Ray does. I know that Ray is always checked on here.

The aides came in to change Ray's bedding. And the nurse was going to treat the open holes in his stomach. When she lifted the top blankets, he was soaked. I never checked that because he seemed exhausted and I didn't want to disturb him. When I came back into the room after Ray was changed, he was turned to face the door and seemed less agitated. That must have been it. He didn't like being wet. It's so hard to know what he needs.

Still, Ray just wanted to hold my hand. He didn't want his zebra or his pink dog. All he wanted was his hand in mine. I was only going to stay for an hour and a half, but I didn't want to leave until Ray fell asleep. He just got settled down and back to sleep when the beeper went off on his IV pole. Laura came in to fix it. Then, a few minutes later, she came in to give him more morphine. Then, a little while later, he had to have a shot to dry up the secretions in his stomach, a treatment left over from last weekend when he had the bowel obstruction.

Three hours after I got there, Ray finally fell blissfully asleep. I quietly, though reluctantly, left him. If I had no job, no family, I would have stayed with him twenty-four hours a day, but, in reality, this whole thing has become so stressful that I fear I may have a heart attack. I'm still getting chest pains. I'm in such a quandary. I want to be with Ray, but I have to limit my stay. I have to save myself for when his end is near so that my family can be with him 24-7.

I got home about 9:30 PM, and needed comfort food. I made a bag of microwave popcorn, to which Mike added another bag of microwave popcorn and half a stick of butter. "We can't eat all of this," I said, even though I wanted to cram the whole thing into my mouth.

"That's okay, Paul's friends will be coming over. They can finish it," he said. There was no popcorn left for Paul's friends. I ate it all and fell asleep in the recliner with no medication to relax me. I haven't done that in months.

February 19, Sunday

The Knights of Columbus had a Mass at our church this morning with a breakfast afterward at their hall. I had to get out of the house, away from family, and amongst people that weren't in the midst of sorrow. I went to Mass and the breakfast alone.

I sat with my friend, Donna, and her husband, Elliott. I filled her in on what had been going on for the past two weeks. Elliott just dotes on me, and Donna is a sympathetic, non-judgmental ear. I love them both dearly, and really appreciate it that they call once in a while to see how I'm doing.

I talked to Donna about feeling guilty that I see little of Paul nowadays. He sleeps most of the day, goes to night classes, and then goes out afterwards. Ray needs me. He's just a baby in a man's body. Paul is a man now, and doesn't want his mommy anymore. Still, I love having heart-to-heart discussions with him and, presently, I'm not doing that. I don't see why I feel guilty. Paul's okay with that. He knows that I need to be with Ray. If Paul needs me, I'll be there for him. I'm so torn right now.

Today I had off from seeing Ray, but still I didn't have a chance to relax. My dad called and said that he had to get a birth certificate for Raymond. I knew it was easy to get one, but I didn't know exactly where to get it. I'll call Mike's sister, Katherine. She did a lot of work for a lawyer who handled family court.

Then Dad had other questions. "For Lynn, this one form is asking for her education. Are we complicating things by appointing a standby and an alternate guardian? [Lynn and me]? Do they have to ask for background checks on them?" he asked.

I looked through all of the papers that I had (I'm making copies of everything that involves Ray), and nowhere did it have a form that asked for a background on Lynn or me. "No, Dad it doesn't ask for that," I replied.

"Well, this form I'm filling out asks for her education. She went to a two-year business school right?" he asked.

"Yeah," I said.

"I listed Raymond's assets as about $1,500," he said.

I'm thinking, why do they want to know that? I got my answer.

"We're going for guardianship of his person and property," he continued.

"Dad, what could he have that we would want? Don't you think that the home will give us Ray's things? Why would we make things worse by haggling over what little things he has? We don't need them." I couldn't get him to budge on that.

"Here, Mom wants to talk to you," he said.

Mom was actually the most cheerful I've heard in a long time. "I just talked to my sister-in-law, your Aunt Sara," Mom said.

I haven't seen my aunt in more than 20 years. I remember her fondly. I send her a Christmas card every year.

"Aunt Sara is Ray's godmother," she said. I hadn't known that. Mom went on, "I told her what was happening to him, and she was crying. She said, 'I'm such a weak person.'"

I said, "Mom there are a lot of people crying over Ray."

"There are?" she asked.

"Yeah, Mom," I replied. "Don't you remember Chaplain O'Shay? He said that he couldn't sleep because he had been thinking about Ray. Emily told me one day that she went home and cried after seeing Ray. Mom, there are a lot of people out there whose hearts are aching because of what's happening to us."

"Sara feels so bad that she wants to send up money to pay for Ray's legal fees," she said.

"Oh, how nice of her," I said. The world is full of beautiful people who are trying to make our burden more bearable. I don't think that's possible. Only the state can do that, and they're not going to budge.

Mom said, "She, at one time, was going to put Ray in her will. I told her no. What was he going to do with all of her money? She thinks it's nice that you kids still think of her."

All I do is send her a card every year. I didn't realize that made such an impression. I'll have to make it a point of sending more cards and contacting her when this is over.

I hung up the phone, and did my arm stretches. I'm getting tendonitis in my elbow from typing, holding the phone for hours, and playing spider solitaire. I've probably played hundreds of games to relieve my stress since I discovered it on my laptop last week. A doctor once told me that people acquire addictions to make them feel better. Well, right now I'm addicted to comfort food and spider solitaire. What else will I be addicted to before this is over?

Today I talked to Mike's sister, Katherine. Katherine told me how to get a birth certificate, and tomorrow she will ask someone in her office to find the New York State law that guarantees every ward of the state nutrition. I've been asking Emily if she could get me a copy of that law. If people at Northbrook are quoting from that law, someone in that facility must know where to find it. It's been two weeks, and Emily keeps telling me that she has left people notes, yet I still don't have that law in my hands. I see Emily being pulled in so many different directions, so I don't want to pester her too much.

I found the procedure for guardians to withdraw someone from life support and other laws, but nothing that specifically says you cannot take anyone off of nutrition when they're a ward of New York State. From what I understand, I was wrong. My parents can be involved in medical decisions for Ray, except the decision to withdraw life-sustaining treatment. The most important decision of all and my parents can't make it because they are not Ray's guardians.

I try to check the internet for more information every chance I get, but I keep getting drawn to spider solitaire.

February 20, Monday

I have today off from work for President's Day. I want to just sleep all day long, but I can't. I have to do catch up on everything that I couldn't get done last week. My house has clutter in every room, but I never have time to put anything away. Mike and Paul don't mind. They just push it aside and do what they need to do. I don't think I'll be able to really relax for a long, long time, even after Ray passes. What's happening to him haunts me so much that I know I can't let it go after he's gone. I have to get his story out, somehow.

I met my parents at Northbrook at 3:00 PM. I gave them some of the paperwork that we filled out together at their house. They're going to take it to Matt's office tomorrow, and his secretary will type up what she can so that the forms will be in place when Matt gets back to work this next Monday.

Ray was sleeping peacefully. I've never seen him sleep for so long at one time. Is he getting better? I was beginning to doubt how bad the doctors said that he was.

My mother voiced my thoughts, "Does he seem better?"

"Mom, even if Ray's stomach heals, the doctors said that Ray probably won't survive another surgery," I answered. "He's lost two more pounds in these past three weeks. They're supposed to weigh him tonight. Laura said, 'It will be interesting to see if he's lost more weight.'"

I find it hard to believe that he could lose more weight. He has no muscles left. His joints are protruding from the thin layer of skin that's left on his bones.

Ray's stomach is oozing green. His nurse, Laura, said that it's an infection, but it doesn't smell. She said that the antibiotics will help with that. I wonder why they are giving them to him? Who ordered antibiotics, if the medical staff was told that they don't have to initiate any new treatment? I'm getting conflicting answers to my questions. I'm going to stop trying to figure it all out. It's futile. It makes my head spin. I need to save my sanity to help Ray.

Ray's been sleeping for two hours. That's okay, Ray-Ray. It's better that way. I hope that he sleeps the rest of his life away. I just held his hand and watched the DVD, *Finding Nemo*, for the third time.

February 21, Tuesday

Today my nerves are all jangled. Well, more jangled than normal. I had to learn a new job today in a different section of the office. I'm always a wreck when that happens. The uncertainty of having people asking questions and wanting help with things that I may not know about sets my sensitive nerves on edge. Top that off with all that has happened to me and my family in the past four months. It culminated in my being a complete basket case.

The new job wasn't as bad as I thought it would be but, in between that, I had to figure out how to get a birth certificate for Raymond. I called city hall—the big city; not the tiny city in which I lived in, but the one in which I worked.

"Can you tell me how I go about getting a birth certificate for my brother?" I asked.

"You need permission from your brother," the city hall clerk replied.

Here we go again. I'm so tired of constantly explaining Raymond's condition. "He's mentally and physically handicapped," I said.

"Do you have power of attorney?" the clerk asked.

"No," I replied.

"Then you need a letter from your mother and father giving us permission to release the birth certificate to you. We need copies of picture ID from both of them," I was told.

More bureaucratic hoops I have to jump through. I understood the reasoning behind it all, but I'm tired, and my patience is wearing thin.

I had to call my parents to figure out the logistics of getting letters and copies of picture ID from them without me running all over the place. Finally, we decided that they would each write a letter, go over to my house while I was at work, have Mike copy their licenses, and leave the paperwork there. I would get the paperwork and tomorrow go to city hall.

Every time I came back to my desk today, there was a message on my voice mail. Both of my brothers called to see how I was doing. Do I really sound that bad? Maybe I did, but I didn't notice because I'm trying so hard to just keep on going through all of this crap.

During my break today, I was talking to one of the arbitrators with whom I work. He asked how Ray was doing. He tried to justify what was happening, like there is any justification to keeping an innocent person alive and forcing him to endure daily pain. "Well, the state doesn't want to open themselves up to lawsuits," he said.

"What lawsuit would that be if the whole family was in agreement to let my brother pass on? Who would object?" I asked. No answer from him. "By keeping my brother alive, they're opening themselves to a lawsuit for cruel and inhuman treatment. Animals are treated better than my brother is."

"You do have a point there," he agreed.

After I described how Ray was the last time I saw him, the arbitrator asked, "How are you and your family getting through all of this?"

"Well, I guess after awhile you become mentally and physically numb to everything out of survival. Every once in a while, I go out somewhere among friends just to assure myself that there is a better world out there," I told him. "I'm just not in it right now."

He couldn't think of anything to say. What do you say to lessen the pain and turmoil of what my family is going through? I just turned and walked down the hallway, back to my desk.

Later today, I found out that I was wrong. I wasn't numb to what was going on. While I was driving home from work, something triggered my memory of Ray, and I cried the whole way home.

One of my co-workers told me that there was an article in the newspaper about feeding tubes. I looked for it when I got home. It was written by a reverend from a local church. It talked about how feeding tubes were initially meant to get someone through a temporary health problem. They are being used more and more to keep individuals alive indefinitely because people are having a hard time letting go of their loved ones. They think that someone who has food and water withheld is suffering a horrible death. The article said that's a fallacy because, usually, when it comes time to make the decision to put in a feeding tube, that person is already malnourished and dehydrated and won't even feel the starvation and thirst that rapid withdrawal from nourishment brings. It's not like they were perfectly healthy and suddenly had to stop eating and drinking.

The article also mentioned that the introduction of the feeding tube has brought with it a whole new gamut of medical and legal problems. It mentioned legislation that was recommended in 1992 and culminated in the Family Health Care Decisions Act, which hasn't been passed yet by the New York State Legislature. I think that this is what I've been looking for. I took down the web sites mentioned in the article. I'll have to take this information and see what I can find on the internet, if I can restrain myself from playing spider solitaire.

I was talking to my sister, Lynn, today. I told her, "I'd like to testify in front of the state legislature and tell them how their laws are not helping people. They're just causing more suffering. I wish that they could see Ray. I'd love to take pictures, then shove them in their faces." I knew if they saw pictures they'd see that Raymond was a real person. A person just like them. A person who's just as important as they are.

I have to be persistent in finding out which politicians to contact to tell them what is happening to Ray, but right now I have to hold Ray's hand. It sounds so simplistic, but isn't that all anyone needs— someone to hold their hand and help them through the bad times? I don't mind at all. The easiest part of this whole ordeal is spending time with Ray. I just held his hand and watched Mike's DVD with 101 cartoon classics, while the snow swirled around outside of Ray's window.

February 22, Wednesday

I talked to my brother from Massachusetts, who said that Mom talked to Ray's nurse, who said that Ray's liver and kidneys are failing. Ray's nurse last night didn't say anything about that. She said that he was weighed and was 74 pounds. He had actually gained weight. Ray just continues to confound everyone.

I called Lynn, and she said that she would ask tonight what to expect. Will he bloat up or turn yellow? Maybe we'll get an idea of how much longer he will live.

My friend at work said that once the liver and kidneys fail, a person's days are numbered. After hearing that, I decided to call the nurses' station to find out for myself. The line was busy.

I called Ray's room. Mom answered.

"It's your pain-in-the-butt daughter," I said. I introduce myself that way on the phone now.

"Pat?" she asked.

"Do you have more than one daughter who's a pain in the butt? Anyway, your son told me that Ray's blood levels are elevated. What does that mean?" I asked.

"I don't know," she responded.

"Well, did you talk to Dr. Patel?" I asked.

"Well, she filled out the forms," she said.

What was she talking about? "What forms, Mom?" I asked.

"The forms for guardianship," she replied.

What did that have to do with this conversation? I figured that I wasn't going to get any information from Mom.

"Okay, Mom. Goodbye," I said.

She said, "They're talking about putting Ray in his chair today."

I thought that she was losing it, maybe from the stress, so I humored her. "Really?" I said. "That's great. Okay, Mom, goodbye."

I finally got through to the nurses' station. Nancy said that Ray's blood levels are elevated. I don't know exactly what levels she's talking about, but my brain hurts too much to try to figure anything out anymore. She didn't know why they were up. It could be for a number of reasons, but if they continue to go up, it could be a sign of failure.

It's amazing how information can get so screwed up after it's gone through so many people. Okay, now I knew exactly what was going on with Ray. Well, no, I didn't. At least I knew that they didn't know if his liver and kidneys were failing.

Nancy wanted to give me some good news. She said, "If you had asked me last week, I would have said Ray was a goner, but today he's in his wheelchair, smiling away." So, Mom wasn't losing it. Nancy went on, "When he went by the nurse's station, he waved at us." I've never seen Ray wave at anyone, but I let that one go. "I guess he's made comebacks before," she added.

"Yeah, I keep asking him, Ray what is going on?" I joked.

"Well, the main thing we'll be facing is if his PICC line fails. I'm amazed that it's still working," she said.

"I suppose Ray has some grand plan," I said. "We just don't know what it is."

"I suppose, but he looks good today. We have him on an antibiotic for his sepsis, but it's toxic to the tissues," she said. The more I learn, the more upset I get.

"Why would you give an antibiotic like that?" I asked.

"Sepsis is so resistant to antibiotics. This is the only one that seems to work. It's only supposed to be temporary," she replied.

"I knew that there was a good reason," I said. She had such patience and never seemed to mind answering my endless questions. "Thank you so much for your time," I finished.

"That's all right," she said kindly, but I bet that she was glad to get me off of the phone.

February 24, Friday

Normally, I'd be thrilled that it's Friday. It's the end of the work week, the beginning of the weekend, and tomorrow I can sleep in; but every day seems the same now. I sleep in on the weekends, but I wake up just as tired as I do during the work week.

Dr. O'Conner hasn't filled out his report for guardianship yet. I was assured by the director of Northbrook that Dr. O'Conner has Ray's best interests at heart. If he does, then why is he holding up the paperwork that we need to gain guardianship of Ray and end his suffering? It was physically given to him and also faxed to him. He's been to Northbrook twice since it was given to him, and still it's not filled out.

Today it was my turn to see Ray. When I got to Northbrook at 4:30 PM, my parents were waiting patiently in Ray's room for Emily to get the paperwork from Dr. O'Conner. They were worn out and just wanted to go home. Dr. O'Conner was physically at Northbrook today. All he had to do was to fill out the few questions on the four pages of the guardianship papers. Basically, all the paperwork asked for was what Dr. O'Conner's qualifications were to be able to determine Ray's mental and physical capacity, what Ray's disabilities were, and whether Ray was fit to appear at a hearing in court.

Emily was flitting around, I think trying to admit someone. Mom, Dad, and I stood patiently outside the TV and dining room area waiting for Emily to finish. Finally, Emily was done. She came up to us. "Dr. O'Conner is here, but he has a patient who is failing. I tried. I really tried. He said that he would fill out the paperwork on Monday."

I didn't believe this. "Emily, let's be serious. Do you really think that he will do that?" I asked her. She rolled her eyes.

Then Mom, Dad, and I started discussing whether another doctor could fill out the paperwork. Maybe a doctor from the town that Ray's group home was in could do it, or maybe one of the doctors in the medical group who took care of Ray when he was in the home.

Emily asked, "Do you want me to get a blank report and give it to you? I make copies of everything. The worst that could happen if you get another doctor to fill it out is you'll end up with three reports."

Something told me that we wouldn't. If Dr. O'Conner hadn't filled out his report by now, that meant he didn't care about what happened to Ray.

Then I thought, why should we have to go looking for a doctor who wasn't currently treating Ray? Why was Dr. O'Conner making it difficult for us? So, I told a little white lie, but, hey, Dr. O'Conner was jerking us around.

"We have everything in place, Emily," I said. "We have all of the forms that we need to go ahead with the guardianship proceedings, except for Dr. O'Conner's. His is the only one that we need. He is the one holding us up."

If he was really concerned about his patients, he could take a few minutes of time from his busy schedule to fill in a few lines.

Emily let out a big sigh and said, "Let me see what I can do." I knew that if anyone could perform a miracle, she could.

Mom and Dad left, and I went to Ray's room to hold his hand while he dozed. Apparently, he had been put in his wheelchair yesterday and delighted everyone with his smile for about half an hour. Then he tired out. It was about 2½ hours before the aides could put him back to bed. It must have exhausted him, because my parents said that he slept all day today.

About 30 minutes passed, and Emily came into Ray's room with a folder in her hand and a smile on her face. Victory was hers. She had stood by Dr. O'Conner and offered bribes until he had relented and filled out the report.

"Thank you, so much!" I told her. I beamed at her and gave her a big bear hug. Who's going to perform miracles for me when Ray's gone from this place? I'm really going to miss these people. In the folder were the signed, notarized copies of Dr. Patel's and Dr. O'Conner's reports, the two release records from West End Hospital, and Ray's admission record to Northbrook Nursing Home. God bless that woman.

Mike came to meet me with chicken wings—my request. As soon as he entered the room, Ray perked up and gave Mike the biggest smile that I've seen in months. He stayed awake for the entire two hours that Mike and I were there. Every time Mike looked at Ray, Ray would grin from ear to ear.

"Sure, I sit here and hold his hand for hours, and all I get is a slight smile, then he falls asleep. As soon as you walk into the room, he's wide awake and smiling from ear to ear. I wish you could come more often," I said to Mike.

As I sat there, I thought, how are we going to be able to make the decision to take Ray off of life support if he's smiling at us? I wonder if he's getting better. Such turmoil this funny little man is causing inside me.

Two aides, whom I don't remember seeing before, kept walking by the room. Each time one would pass, they'd poke their head in and check on Ray. "Is everything okay?" they'd ask. Everyone in this place loves Raymond.

Laura was on duty today. She came in several times even after attending to his IVs and medications. "Now, if you need anything, if he feels uncomfortable, you tell me." Ray has no idea how many people care about him.

February 26, Sunday

The phone rang at 9:00 AM. This isn't good, I thought to myself. No one calls me this early on a Sunday. I got a terrible, sinking feeling in my stomach. It was Lynn. She was with Ray at Northbrook this morning. She had been there last night, and Ray had coughed up a big hunk of phlegm, then threw up green stuff.

"He had that scared look in his eyes again," she said. "I asked the nurse when the last time he got morphine was, and she went out to check the chart. He hadn't had morphine all day. It took two hours for the morphine to kick in and for him to settle down. I told the nurse that I was thinking of staying overnight. That nurse asked me, 'Why, is he uncomfortable?'"

Ray had just thrown up phlegm and green stuff. Wouldn't you be scared and uncomfortable if you had a child's mentality and that happened to you? Why is it so hard for people to understand how Ray must be feeling?

Lynn had stayed late last night. After awhile, Ray seemed more comfortable, so she decided to leave and go back early this morning.

Before she left Northbrook, the nurse had asked, "Do you want him to have morphine every three hours?" Lynn didn't know, but thought that he shouldn't go all day without getting it either. So the nurse said that she would write in Ray's chart to give morphine at 12:00 midnight and 6:00 AM. I don't know why the nurses couldn't be more diligent about checking on Ray on the weekends.

Lynn and I were allowing my mom and dad a day off, which meant that we would split today and each stay half the day. "When were you planning on coming down?" Lynn asked me.

I heaved a big sigh, trying not to let Lynn hear it. I don't know why I sighed. I'd spend hours, days, weeks with Ray if that's what he needed.

I answered, "Well, I had planned on 1:00. Do you want me to come earlier?"

"If you're going to stay overnight, won't you want to come later?" she asked.

"You were there late last night and then early this morning. No, you'll be there long enough. I'll come at 1:00 and pack clothes and food in case Ray's bad, then I'll stay overnight. I guess we'll have to take one day at a time," I said.

I still don't trust the staff on weekends. They don't know Ray's history. I just don't feel comfortable leaving Ray alone because of what happened that one weekend when they tried taking Ray to West End twice without discussing it with my family or his regular doctor.

I got to Northbrook about 1:30 PM. Ray was sleeping. He was in a drugged-up stupor. His eyes were rolled up inside his head, with his lids not completely closed. His mouth was wide open. I could hear his breath coursing in and out.

The tall, black nurse practitioner, who I had the discussion about Terry Schiavo with, came into the room before Lynn left to go home.

I said to the nurse practitioner, "Ray's not doing well."

The nurse practitioner looked at Ray. "Really? He's doing better," she said.

What? Lynn said, "Well, he threw up brown stuff this morning." This was news to me. "It looked like old blood."

That's exactly what I thought it was when that happened last weekend when he threw up for two days. The nurse practitioner went on to explain that sometimes the body gets stressed, and that can lead to ulcers. Perhaps Ray has ulcers that are acting up. I wouldn't be surprised if Ray did have ulcers. I wouldn't be surprised if *I* had ulcers.

"Well, he's doing much better than last weekend," she said, trying to make us feel better. Of course he was doing better. He wasn't throwing up every two hours, but that doesn't mean he's doing well.

While the nurse practitioner did Ray's treatment to his stomach, Lynn and I stood in the hallway just outside Ray's room.

Lynn told me, "That nurse practitioner said that his stomach looked horrible. I told her, 'Well, it looks much better than it was at West End.'"

"Yeah, it's not so red," I replied.

"She said that she ordered zinc oxide," Lynn said.

Every time someone different takes care of Ray, they have a different opinion on how to treat him. None of the treatments are going to relieve him. He's so far gone, absolutely nothing will make him better. I suppose it's their way of trying to help him.

Then I remembered. I said, "The other ladies have been putting Maalox on Ray's stomach." Lynn's eyes widened in surprise. "Well, it calms down stomach acid when you take it orally," I said. It made sense to me.

The nurse practitioner was surprised when Lynn passed along that little tidbit of information.

Lynn left, and soon, a loud, heavyset woman came in the room, bellowing, "Hello, Ray," from the doorway. Ray opened his eyes and granted her a smile. I don't feel quite so upset when I see Ray smile. The woman came into the room and sat on the bed. She talked to him for a minute or so, then left.

I checked out Ray's stomach. Even though his treatment was just about 30 minutes ago, the towel that was pressed against his abdomen to catch the drainage from his holes was covered in green *and* brown, something I haven't seen before. It's gross and slimy. I probably shouldn't be touching it, but I have to know what's happening. I probably shouldn't be hugging and kissing someone who has a blood infection, but I have to comfort my brother. My hands are getting raw from washing them so much.

I watched *Finding Nemo* on my laptop again. Ray seemed interested for a few minutes, then slipped in and out of his stupor. Mike will be meeting me down here at about 6:00 PM with a turkey sub.

The world is held at bay when I'm alone with Ray. There's nothing to do but comfort him. The world that has entangled my family into its nightmare seems so far away from Ray's room.

February 27, Monday

Today I was only going to stay about an hour and a half with Ray, but he was so uncomfortable. He was wet, so he was trying to pull himself up, or something. He seemed better after he was changed, but his nurse came in with morphine. We decided to give it to him. He smiled for a while when he heard the music from the *Sound of Music,* then he got that drugged-up stupor look on his face. He still wouldn't go to sleep. I hated to leave him awake and looking so miserable. I stayed until 8:00 PM, way longer than I planned to. I got to see the *Sound of Music* from beginning to end one more time.

I had to go home. Ray was still awake when I left his room. At the nurses' station, I told them my feelings. "I think that the morphine is making Ray ill."

"He's been on morphine a long time," the nurse said.

Okay, so does that mean that he should have gotten sick from it a long time ago? Does that mean that he should look sick every time he gets morphine? I didn't understand what she was getting at, but I was too tired to try to make sense out of it.

"I'm going to give him a suppository," she told me. "I see that he had a bowel movement, but he may have an obstruction again. Maybe he's blocked."

It's so hard taking care of someone who can't tell you anything about how they feel.

I can't stand this limbo that we're being forced into. Waiting and waiting, watching my brother become a skeleton, miserable and suffering and not being able to do a darn thing about it because of the state laws.

When I got home, I prayed that God would take Ray's life. Is that such a horrible thing? As I laid my head on my tear-soaked pillow I prayed that somehow I would find a reason for all of this. That's how I keep my sanity. I wait for God to show me the reason for this happening. If there is no reason, then it's just plain human torture for Ray and my family.

I had a good, gut-wrenching cry. I haven't done that in, oh, a few weeks.

February 28, Tuesday

I get a sinking feeling in the pit of my stomach each time the phone rings, even at work. It's like Pavlov's dogs conditioned to salivate when they hear a bell. I never get any good news when I answer the phone anymore, so now I hear the ring, and I automatically get a feeling of impending doom.

Mike called me to tell me to call Matt at his office. Why didn't he just call my parents? Well, I've been at the center of all of this from the beginning, not by choice, but because I'm the one willing to speak out. So I've been put in charge.

"Matt must have contacted the courts because they were asking why your family wants the guardianship procedure to go through a different county than the one Ray's group home is in," Mike said.

Great—after talking to Matt, I found out that the courts have to have an affidavit signed by my parents which states that Ray resides at Northbrook and will stay there. Where else can he go? His group home won't take him back because he has an IV, and state law says that we can't take his IVs out. He was released by West End Hospital. The only place he can go to is a nursing home, and he's never going to improve enough to get out. Just another glitch in the quagmire of bureaucracy that is supposed to be looking after Ray's best interests.

March 1, Wednesday

I can't believe that February is over. Ray's been at Northbrook since January 26—a month and a few days. I couldn't stop crying at work. The thought of doing this for another month or more is just too much for me.

Ray looked really miserable today. He was trying to turn himself and had a nauseated look on his face. I checked his bed. He had wet himself. Now I know that if he wants to move, it's probably because he's wet. The aides changed him, but when they moved him it must have upset his delicate stomach because he started coughing and gagging like he was going to bring up something. Nothing came out, but he still had a sick look on his face the rest of the night. I couldn't look at him because it made me want to gag, myself.

How much longer are they going to make Ray and my family go through this? This is cruel.

Ray had a fever of 100, not something to get excited about. I talked to Laura, who watches over him like one of her own kids. We can't figure out if his nausea is coming from the morphine, his fever, or what. At this point, morphine is the only pain reliever that they can give besides what he gets from his patch. All we can do is try to figure out if he is in pain, and if he is, give him morphine. Then we can try to control the nausea with other meds.

This week I've seen *Aladdin* and *The Sound of Music* twice. I'm going to know a lot of songs before this is all over. Ray didn't seem too pleased with my singing today. Maybe the next time.

I got a call at home from Laura at about 10:00 PM. Ray's fever has gone up, even though Laura gave him a Tylenol suppository. She called Dr. Patel, who ordered an injection to bring down the fever. When will the suffering end? Laura ended her call with, "I just wanted you to know that Ray is smiling." What a sweetie she is. The angels were with us when Ray was admitted to Northbrook.

March 2, Thursday

I can't stop eating. My bad habits are multiplying. Now they are eating comfort food, chewing gum, and playing spider solitaire. Thank God I can't smoke or drink. I'd be stinking drunk and reeking of smoke all of the time.

I called our attorney's office and spoke to the secretary.

She said, "The affidavit is sitting on my desk to be typed this morning."

"I don't mean to be a pain, but every day this guardianship proceeding is delayed is another day that my brother is suffering," I said.

"I can assure you that I will type it and call your parents to come sign it this morning," she said.

"Do you have any idea, once this affidavit is received, how long before we know when our court date is?" I asked.

"I don't want to answer that because I don't want to give you any false information. I can tell you that the court has all of the other paperwork," she replied. "I'll have Matt call you," she said. "Can I have your name and phone number?"

"Matt knows me, but I can give you my cell phone number," I replied.

I called Dad at home to give him the heads-up that the secretary would be calling him.

Dad called me at about 10:00 AM from Northbrook. "You won't believe it, but Ray is up in his chair, sitting in the TV room, and smiling away. He's watching *Oliver* with the other residents," he told me.

I was amazed. "Wow, he was miserable last night," I said. Ray is baffling us all.

Matt called me at work to tell me that we have a court date on April 6. I can't see Ray lasting that long, but, hey, he's fooled people before. I pray that God will take him before that time. He's suffering so much, except for those rare moments when his gentle smile radiates from his soul.

Today was a very topsy-turvy day for me. Some of it was good, some bad. It snowed all day long in the city where I work. We accumulated about a total of six inches of the white stuff. When I went out to my van, which is parked in an open lot, every other car had piles of snow on it but mine. Mine had absolutely no snow all around it and a triangle-shaped patch of snow on the windshield, measuring about two feet long. One swipe of the windshield wipers took care of that. I took my brush and helped Ginny and one other man I work with get the snow off of their cars. Got to pass the good luck around.

I spoke to Mom after I got home from work, and she said that poor Ray wasn't put back to bed until 2:00 PM. That poor man. Why can't they put him in his chair for about a half hour?

Mom answered my question. "Nancy said she'd get someone to put him back in bed, but then she looked around and said, 'There's no one here. Where did they all go?' And it was a long time before anyone came to put Ray to bed," she told me.

With all the cutbacks in health care these days, none of these facilities have enough help to be attentive. Sure, they take care of the absolute necessities, like administering meds and clean-up a few times a day, but on a day when you have a lot of special-needs patients, there isn't enough time to give each patient individual attention.

Tonight Lynn called and said that when she saw Ray, he was nauseated again. I asked her if he had been given morphine.

Lynn responded, "I asked Laura if he got it, and she said that she would check, but she never told me after that. She gave him something else besides the anti-nausea medicine they've been giving him. He did throw up a few times."

"What color was it this time?" I asked.

"It was green," Lynn informed me.

I'm a sickly person, so I know my infections. "That could mean that he's coughing up phlegm. If it's green, it means infection." When I have a cold, my doctors always ask what color the phlegm is that I cough up. I never can tell them because I can't bring it up to spit it out. I have to swallow it. Now I'm getting sick just thinking about it.

"Laura said that it was bile. But then she said that she thinks the nausea is nature taking its course," Lynn said.

"What does that mean?" I asked.

"Well, she said that he might have pneumonia. And I asked her if she could hear phlegm in his lungs. She said that sometimes you can have pneumonia without the gunk in your lungs. They call it silent pneumonia," Lynn said.

Time will tell what takes Ray's life. Will it be a natural progression that takes him, or will it be up to us to withdraw his nutrition? I thank God for not knowing what our future holds because I would have told God, "Forget it. Do what you want to me, but I'm not going through that."

Lynn will be gone all weekend, from Friday to Sunday. It's going to be a long weekend for me.

March 3, Friday

I almost made it through my workday without any calls about Ray. I was just thinking how peaceful it was. Actually the day was getting boring, but in a nice way. I'd like boring for a long, long time.

Then my dad called. "I'm at Northbrook. I was served today," he told me.

"What?" I responded.

"I was served with a notice that Raymond is to appear in court. It's addressed to Raymond and some name that I don't recognize. I think he's the director of the regional NYS DDSO," Dad said.

"Wait," I told him. I pulled out my envelope that I always carry with me that has correspondence from the regional NYS DDSO and all the phone numbers from everyone I've talked to since the beginning of this whole mess.

I pulled out the correspondence from Joe Griffin on the letterhead of the regional NYS DDSO. The name that Dad said was at the top, under the director of the regional NYS DDSO. During this whole time, the director has never tried contacting any of my family.

Now, you might think that in a sad, sad situation like this one, he would have made an attempt.

"How is Raymond?" I asked.

"He seems uncomfortable," Dad replied.

"Check his bed and see if it's wet," I instructed. "Every time I've been with him and he's been trying to pull himself up, it's because he's wet. He gets a miserable look on his face."

Dad yelled to Mom to check Ray's bed. Sure enough, he was wet. Poor thing. He can't tell us what's wrong, so we, in our desire to make him feel comfortable, are drugging him up with morphine that I think is making him nauseated, and all that's bothering him is a wet bed. Problem solved. Or so I think.

"Mike is working with Matt at the fish fry at the Knights of Columbus tonight," I said. "He can ask him. It's probably just a formality that they have to go through. Don't worry, Dad. Matt will have everything under control."

I finished my work day and went to see Ray. He was hot, hot, hot, like he had a fever.

Laura had off. There was another nurse whom I had seen before who usually works on the pediatric ward on the other side of Ray's floor. She was very nice, but not as attentive as Laura.

I got a smile for about the first half hour, and then Ray went sour. He scrunched up his face and started to cry for a few minutes. He stopped and dozed off. When he woke up, he started coughing and choking as if he had to bring up something and couldn't. All that came out of his mouth was saliva. Then he stopped, but he was breathing very heavily. It was strange, but he would breathe in fine and then breathe out hard as if he had a hard time getting the air out of his lungs. I thought that he might be getting pneumonia, but when you have a chest cold, don't you usually have a hard time breathing in?

The aide came in to change the packing around Ray's stomach. I could hear him coughing again. When I came back in, he was doing that gagging thing, and I heard gurgling in his throat as if he needed to bring something up. The aide asked me if I wanted her to get a nurse. The nurse came in and saw him coughing. "Well, I can give him something for nausea," she said. She left for awhile.

I started planning what to do if I have to stay overnight again. I couldn't leave him in that condition. The nurse asked if it might be good to raise the head of the bed. Dummy me, why didn't I think of that?

Ray was asleep by the time the nurse returned with a few syringes and a bag to hook up to his IV. I'm nosy, so I asked her, "What is all that?" It was a syringe to flush Ray's PICC line. The bag was his Dilantin for seizures, which was to be hooked up to his PICC line next. Before that was done, a syringe of anti-nausea medicine was put into the PICC line.

"Ray had morphine this afternoon at about 3:00," the nurse said.

"Well, that might explain the nausea. I still think he might be having a reaction to the morphine," I said. But he didn't have that nauseated or drugged-up look on his face like he usually does a few hours after he has morphine.

I wish I was a psychic who could contact someone in heaven who might know what's going on. Are we adding to Ray's misery with all of these drugs, or are we really helping him?

Ray continued in a blissful slumber for a long time. I decided not to stay the night. Lynn is going away for the weekend, and it's going to be a long one without her. I needed to save myself for whatever comes.

I went to the Knights of Columbus just for one drink. I sat at the bar and didn't even care if I talked to anyone or if anyone talked to me. I want to get drunk out of my mind, but I drove, and tomorrow I have to go see Ray, which means that I have to get up early and do as much as I can around the house before I leave.

A friend, whom I hadn't talked to since December, asked how Ray was and if he was still in the hospital. "He's never going back home," I told her. "He's in Northbrook, and that's where he'll stay. We're going for guardianship so that we can have treatment stopped. Until then, because he's a ward of the state and doesn't have a guardian, they have to keep him alive."

She didn't have a reply to that news. She just wished me well and left.

Donna called me down to the end of the bar to see a brochure on the next show that she wants to book at the Knights. It was an Elvis impersonator. We listened to his CD. I started thinking about decorations for the show. Maybe his name in lights as a backdrop. I love decorating. For a few moments, I was thinking about something not tied to Ray.

March 4, Saturday

My parents were going to see Ray about 12:00 today and would stay a few hours. I went in at about 3:00 PM and stayed into the night. They were going in late tomorrow and were staying a bit longer and giving me tomorrow off.

Ray was smiling away when I got to Northbrook. I guess they had brought dogs through to interact with the residents. Ray loved the dogs. He didn't get morphine at all today. I saw no nausea, only hiccups. I didn't see any terrified look in his eyes. He did scowl for a while and rub his face. He was tired, and he had a fever again today. He's been running one off and on for as long as I can remember. I don't know why the sepsis in his blood or his infected PICC lines haven't taken him yet. He must have some unfinished business, or we have something we're supposed to do before he passes. I wish I knew what it was.

The time passes quickly in Ray's room. It's never boring. Today, while Ray was sleeping, I read some information on state laws that I printed out—laws about guardianship and making medical decisions for incapacitated loved ones. The information is hard for me to understand. It's filled with legal mumbo jumbo that I have to read three and four times before I comprehend it. I'm learning a lot about laws and how they are passed in New York State. Maybe God plans for me to get involved in politics when this is over.

Ray and I passed the time watching the movie, *Garfield*, and every episode of *The Beverly Hillbillies*. I set my laptop close to him on an adjustable bed-stand in his room. His eyes lit up, and he smiled from ear to ear when he heard the theme song from *The*

Beverly Hillbillies. This week I've seen *The Wizard of Oz, Garfield, The Sound of Music,* all of the episodes of *The Beverly Hillbillies,* and about 50 cartoon classics. Not bad, but I'll have to start renting tapes or DVDs. I'm already getting sick of the ones Ray has, and I have a feeling that we'll go through many more DVDs before this is over. Ray fell blissfully asleep, and I snuck out of his room at 7:45 PM.

March 6, Monday

Lynn called me tonight from Ray's room. I get an update every day from whoever sees Ray. I can't handle not knowing how he's doing. It's like my own child being sick.

"Well, Pat, he's smiling away," she reported. "When Laura came into the room, he smiled from ear to ear and took her hand and patted it." That's Ray's way of showing affection. "It looks like he's trying to pull her on top of him." He just loves Laura.

"See, I bet he didn't get his morphine today," I said.

"No, he got it at 3:00," Lynn said. Well, that blows my theory. "He has a fever, so Laura gave him a Tylenol suppository. He doesn't like that."

"If you did like that, there'd be something wrong with you," I responded.

I hung up the phone and decided to stop trying to figure out what's happening to Ray. I'll never figure it out. There's no way that I can control anything concerned with Ray. I just have to accept that whatever is happening is in God's hands and have faith that in time God will show me why Ray had to endure such suffering.

March 7, Tuesday

I haven't seen Ray for two days. On the days that I don't see him, I get antsy if I don't get a report from Lynn or Mom and Dad.

Today I ordered the report written by the group that was formed by the state legislature, who recommend changes in the law regarding withdrawal of life-sustaining treatment 14 years ago. From those recommendations the Family Health Care Decisions Act was put together. This act was put before the New York State legislature for the past three years, and it has yet to pass both houses. The Assembly has been working on the bill this year, but hasn't put it up for a vote yet. The Senate hasn't acted on the bill at all this year. What is wrong with the politicians in Albany? It's not like this issue is something minor that happens only occasionally.

I also found a site that has stories of people who have gone through just what we are going through. How can lawmakers make innocent people like Ray suffer so much? The laws are cruel. They're outdated. There is no reason that I can see why it is allowed to continue.

I have names of people to contact for advice on what to do to make sure that attention is drawn to this issue. But I still can't find any law that states that nutrition is guaranteed to wards of the state.

This week I will see Ray today and Wednesday. Lynn saw him yesterday and will go again on Thursday and Friday. I don't know what the weekend will entail. I can't think too far ahead. My brain goes to mush when I do.

When I got to Ray's room today, I was so hoping to see him smiling like Lynn did yesterday. Instead, he was growling and crying like he does when something is wrong. He had that nauseated look on his face, and it wasn't long before he started gagging like he was going to throw up.

"Let's put on *The Beverly Hillbillies*, Ray-Ray. You always liked them," I said. I took out my laptop and set it up to watch *The Beverly Hillbillies*. He looked at it but still had that sick look on his face. Then he fell asleep. Soon, he started snoring. He's whipped today. Dad said he was told that Ray was in his chair this morning. I wonder if he was in it for hours again.

The employees here are extra loud today, and it isn't even bothering Ray. He's just snoring away. Dad called me to see how Ray was doing and to inquire about stuff that Joe Griffin brought to Northbrook.

I reported, "Yeah, he brought the electric razor, which I put a tag on, and some t-shirts that were being given to the social worker to be taken down to the laundry to have a tag put on. That takes a couple of days."

"Joe Griffin says he thinks it's a state law that says they have to keep him alive," Dad said.

"Yeah, it is, Dad, but guardians have rights regarding that," I said. "Emily wasn't on the floor when I came in, so I couldn't ask her. We have time to find that out."

"Okay," my dad said, and hung up.

Darn. I completely forgot to ask my dad about his ear. He had cancer taken off of it today. Mom and Dad had to cancel a lot of their doctors' appointments since Ray has been in the hospital. I convinced my parents that they couldn't put them on hold indefinitely. Somehow we'd have to work out the logistics of them going to their appointments and someone being with Ray.

While Ray sleeps I've been reading the laws regarding life support and how it can be withdrawn. As far as I understand, if you haven't expressed your will or cannot express your will, New York State mandates that everything possible should be done to keep you alive. If the person is mentally retarded like Raymond is, and you obtain guardianship through the surrogate courts in regard to making medical decisions, you can make the decision to withdraw nutrition.

How ridiculous. We have to watch Ray suffer day after day until my parents gain guardianship of their own child, which they have to pay an exorbitant amount of money to obtain, because Ray hasn't been appointed a guardian to make decisions for him, even though my parents have been doing it all along. The bottom line is this: if the state is looking after you, you're out of luck if you can't speak for yourself and have a terminal illness that causes you pain and suffering. They're going to do everything possible to continue your suffering until you die from something God-awful that they can't control—like infection or pneumonia or cancer—or until your heart stops and there's a do-not-resuscitate order. If there isn't an order, they'll resuscitate you time and again so that your suffering can continue. This is looking after your best interests the New York State way.

I was going to leave, but Ray woke up after sleeping for an hour. He looked miserable again. I just sat and held his hand. Ray's nurse for the night came into the room. "Aww, how sweet," she said when she saw us holding hands. She mustn't see that often in this place. I thought of how sad it was that some of these residents have to spend their final days with no one to hold their hand.

Ray started crying out again. The aides changed him and flipped him over so that he faced the door. He seemed better after that. Maybe he was in pain because of the way he was positioned. The nurse talked me into leaving at about 8:30.

"You have to go to work tomorrow, don't you?" she inquired.

"Yes. I'm used to it. I hate to leave him like this," I replied.

"He seems better now. You go home and get some rest," she said.

Oh, how I needed rest. I can't take many more days like this.

March 8, Wednesday

Mom called me twice from Northbrook to tell me how Ray was doing. She was there by herself today because Dad wasn't feeling well. I think she just needed someone to talk to. Being a mother myself, I can only imagine what she must be feeling in her heart when she sees her son suffering so much.

Mom told me that Ray was uncomfortable and crying out a lot today. It's my night to see him. When he's like that, it just drains me.

I typed in my laptop and played one game of spider solitaire in the Northbrook parking lot to compose myself before I went in to see Ray. Am I being a bad sister because I can't take Ray's crying anymore? I parked in the overnight parking lot because I wasn't sure if I'd have to be spending the night with Ray. I entered through the back door. There was security sitting at the podium just inside the door.

"You need to sign in," he said to me. "Do you know how to get to the facility?"

Now, I know I've seen him before. He mustn't be able to place me.

"Yes, I've been coming here for quite a few weeks now; almost six," I responded. Has it only been six weeks? It feels like a lifetime since Ray came to Northbrook.

When I got to Ray's room, he was dozing. He woke up when he heard me come in the room. He was trying to pull himself up, but he's too weak to flip over anymore. His head was off the pillow, and he looked so uncomfortable that I tried to lift his head and shove the pillow under it. He let out a high-pitched noise, halfway between a scream and cry.

"Oh, I'm not going to move you Ray. There, I'm done. Now you can calm down," I said.

He must have been drugged up, or the fever was sapping his energy, because he wakes up if there's any noise and then goes right back to sleep. I'm not going to turn on the TV or try to hold his hand for now. It's nice to see him blissfully sleeping away. I'm not going to disturb that. I'll just eat, play spider solitaire, and read the TV manual to see if I can figure out how to make the DVD player work. It's been broken for weeks.

When I was done with that, I read about the Family Health Care Decisions Act. Right now, in New York State, adults who have clear minds must have their wishes in writing regarding end-of-life sustaining treatment before they become incapacitated. It must be either on a state-recognized Health Care Proxy Form or in a signed, notarized statement. If a person's wishes were expressed orally, the family has to go to court and prove with "clear and convincing evidence" what their incapacitated loved one's wishes were. If there is no proof, the loved ones have no right to make decisions regarding withdrawal of treatment. What a bunch of malarkey. Missouri is the only other state in the union that doesn't give families automatic rights when their loved ones become incapacitated.

When Ray is gone, I'd like to start a letter-writing campaign to the legislators to urge them to pass that law, the Family Health Care Decisions Act. I'd like to do more than just urge them. I'd like to show them pictures of how Ray is suffering. I want them to feel what Ray and my family went through. But I'm not going to persuade them if I rant and rave and shove shocking pictures in front of their faces. Still, I have to do something.

Lynn's friend suggested that we start a web site that people can log onto and, with a click, send letters to their legislators. What a great idea, but I don't have a clue how to do that. Lynn and I will have to figure it out when this is all over.

March 10, Friday

Lynn called me last night to tell me that the nurse told her that Ray's antibiotics stopped the day before yesterday. I don't know why no one told us. Wouldn't that have been a good thing to know?

Lynn said, "I asked her how long it would be before Ray passes, and she said about a week, but Ray's such a fighter it wouldn't surprise her if he lasted longer."

"Lynn, there's nothing left of him. How can he last longer?" I asked.

"I know," she said. "Well, Mom and Dad are going to talk to Nancy tomorrow."

"I just don't want him to die alone," I said. I couldn't think of anything more inhumane than poor Ray dying alone after all that he's going through.

I talked to Nancy today, and she said that nothing with Ray has changed.

Are people lying now? I don't understand. Why is the head floor nurse saying that nothing has changed even though Ray's nurse has said that his antibiotics have stopped? Why are we always being left in the dark?

I don't know who is on our side or who is just trying to protect their butts. I believe Ray's nurse, and I felt like the director of Northbrook and Nancy were on our side, but now I don't know. Why can't they just be honest with us? I feel betrayed. I think that everyone all around has screwed up and no one wants to fess up.

I'm not going to ask questions anymore. I've gone through too much for too long to continue this struggle. I thought that I would never get like this, that I would never give up a fight if I knew I was right, but I just don't have the strength anymore. I'm just going to be by Ray's side and accept whatever happens.

I just want Ray to pass peacefully, like he should have done months ago. The poor thing, it was up to us as a society to take care of him, and we have failed him. We've all failed miserably.

March 11, Saturday

It's a beautiful day today. I woke up, and the sun was shining, and it's warm enough to go outside with only a sweatshirt on. Spring is coming extra early this year. I had tea while sitting on my bench in my garden, a ritual with which I love to start the day. I just sit and talk to my dead sister, Janet, to God, and to the angels.

My poor angels must be sorry that they've been assigned to me. I start each prayer to them with, "I'm sorry to bother you again, but once more I'm asking for your help..." I ask them to give me strength to get through another day, and they haven't failed me yet. The only way that I've gotten through all of these months is because my angels have carried me through the days that I couldn't have survived on my own.

I felt so peaceful sitting there on my bench in my garden, but I could only sit for a little while. I have so much that I need to do before I go to see Ray today. I'm giving my parents the day off, which means that I'll be going to see Ray in the early afternoon and staying until after dinner, unless he's bad. Then I'll stay longer. I have to re-pack my overnight bag and put it in my car again. The end is nearing, even though the staff is not conveying it; just Laura, who is passing along information the best that she can.

I bought six helium balloons at the dollar store. The one that Ray's roommate from West End gave him is deflated and stuck to the bulletin board in his room with a tack. I gave three balloons to the third-floor staff, just for the heck of it. I saw them later, tied to the wall railing near the nurses' station. I got a big smiley one for Ray's room. He probably won't even notice it, but, hopefully, it'll cheer up whoever else is in the room.

When I got to Ray's room, he was crying out and looked miserable. I went to the nurses' station and asked the nurse, one whom I had only seen a couple of times before, if it was close to Ray's time for morphine.

"I gave it to him twice today, and I gave him a Tylenol suppository. He just got the second dose of morphine about half an hour ago," the nurse told me.

I knew that Ray must have been bad because it was just 2:00 PM and he already had had two doses of morphine. A pad was on the floor by his bed, which I hadn't seen for weeks, so he must have been moving a lot. There was a towel by his head, so he must have either thrown up or was gagging like he was going to.

Ray seems strong today. He kept trying to turn over to his other side. After about an hour, he dozed off and on. There was a lot of commotion in the hallways today. Emily, the social worker, was admitting a new patient. She came in to see Ray. "How's Ray today?" she yelled into the room before she entered.

"Not so good today," I replied. "We're not going to get any smiles. Hey, why are you working on a Saturday?"

"We have to work at least one Saturday a month. How's everything going with Ray; you know, the guardianship stuff?" she asked.

"Well, we have a court date for April 6. If there's a cancellation, they'll try to fit us in sooner, but I don't think that will happen," I responded.

"I saw that Joe. That man; is he from the group home? Well, I saw him the other day, and I wondered what he's doing around here," Emily said.

"Joe Griffin? He's Ray's Medicaid case manager. He comes in periodically. It might be every week. I know that he brings in things from the group home for Ray; you know, like clothes and his razor," I told her.

I knew by her questions that she didn't trust Joe. I had to defend him. He was my only ally from New York State. "He's okay," I said. "This whole thing with Ray is upsetting to him."

"Well, I just wanted to stop in to see Ray," Emily said. She's a wonderful person—so full of pep and so loud. In fact it seemed like everyone today was peppy; even the man collecting garbage was loud and very talkative. Maybe it was because he was drinking too much caffeine. I saw him take swigs out of a coffee cup every few minutes.

Ray got fussy again after a few hours, then he must have tired himself out again. Lynn called to see how he was doing.

"Well, Lynn he doesn't appear to me to be any weaker or sicker than the last time I saw him. In fact, today he seems more wide awake. The last few times I saw him, he did nothing but sleep. Today he keeps trying to flip over when he's not sleeping," I told her.

"I don't know," Lynn said. "If he's not getting antibiotics, if he still has infection—which he probably does—shouldn't he be running a fever? Laura said that he didn't have a fever yesterday."

"Well, he doesn't have a fever today, either," I said. "He felt really warm when I came in, but the nurse came in and stuck a thermometer under Ray's armpit—as if you'd get a true reading when he has no meat on his bones for any heat to come from. She said that he had no fever."

This whole thing is perplexing me. What in God's name is happening here? Is Ray getting worse, or is he going to linger on for weeks or even months?

Nothing is happening that Nancy said would probably happen. She said that he probably wouldn't last for the three-month time limit that they give people to be on the artificial nutrition because he would probably get a blood infection, which he has, and it hasn't taken him. Or his PICC lines would probably become infected, which they have, and the infection hasn't taken him. Or he would get pneumonia, which his nurse said that he probably has, and that hasn't taken him, either.

Does he still have all of these infections? We can't be sure because they don't want to test for them. If they find them, they may be forced to treat them or be held liable for not treating them. Why would they get in trouble for not treating a man who has no hope of getting better? This is what the screwy laws in New York State have forced this facility and my family to go through. No wonder people are leaving this state in droves.

Ray was wearing me out with his crying and moaning and moving and pulling on my hand and scratching me and pinching me. This went on for about two hours after he got his third dose of morphine. He finally went to sleep at 8:45 PM. Actually, I think he passed out. I snuck out without waking him. Over six hours of watching an innocent's senseless agony. I can't take much more of this. I say that every day, and every day somehow I get through it.

March 12, Sunday

I wrote my health care proxy today and read it to Mike. I begged Mike to write his. I don't want to have to go through the same thing with him as I'm going through with Ray. I hope to God that the state passes that law this year so that we don't need health care proxies.

Mike laughed at me when I read the part I put in the proxy about willing to donate any organs except those whose removal will scar my face. I felt really stupid, until I remembered the woman from Europe who recently had a face transplant. "Do you remember that woman who had a face transplant? How would you like to see my face on someone else?" I asked. End of discussion.

Ray is an obsession with me. I called my parents in Ray's room to see how he's doing. They told me that he could have his morphine every three hours now. Yesterday he went for at least six hours without getting it. Why didn't the nurse on duty come down to Ray's room to ask if I wanted him to have morphine when she heard him yelling so loudly? I had to go looking for her. Well, I'll be more diligent with Ray's morphine from now on.

March 13, Monday

I just remembered today that I missed my friend's daughter's baby shower on Saturday. I feel badly, but I'm just too tired to try to juggle everything. Tonight I spent cooking. I try to cook ahead so that, when I'm not home for dinner, Mike and Paul can eat something decent. I try to keep up with the laundry. I try to keep up with the housework. I try. I really try, but it's so overwhelming. Thank God that Paul is old enough to take care of himself.

Mary called me for an update on Ray. She's so worried that if we take him off of everything he'll suffer. "If you take him off of his nutrition and water, his kidneys will shut down," she lamented.

"Mary, that's a natural part of dying, unless you die suddenly," I said. "I watched Mike's dad die. His systems shut down. He died very peacefully. We're not going to let Ray suffer any more than he is now."

I wish that Mary wouldn't listen to anyone else. No one else has talked to our attorneys or doctors. I wish other people would keep their opinions to themselves and stop making Mary worry any more than she is.

March 15, Wednesday

Today Ginny asked me jokingly if I'm looking forward to seeing Ray. I never mind going there. It's heartbreaking, but I would feel even worse if I wasn't seeing him. It's like spending time with my own child. In fact, I keep calling him "Paul" by mistake when I talk to others about him.

When I got off the elevator on Ray's floor tonight, I got a rare glimpse of one of the little boys from the children's ward on the other side of the floor from Ray's ward. He was walking on his own and looked okay to me. How sad to be a little boy and not be living in a house with a family. How sad to be a little boy and living in a nursing home. Nursing homes are so depressing to me. Maybe when this is over I can do something to help those kids on that floor.

Laura calls Ray "The Mystery Man." I asked her today, "Is it my imagination, or is he getting skinnier?"

"As a matter of fact, he's gained weight, if you can believe it," she said. They weighed him again, recently, and he had gained three pounds.

"Where?" I asked. I took his arm and put my thumb and middle finger around it near his elbow, and they almost touched. His arm is now as big around as my wrist.

Laura shrugged her shoulders. "That's why he's 'The Mystery Man,'" she said. "You just let me know if you need anything. Come get me if he gets uncomfortable, and I'll give him morphine." She left the room.

He has no fever today. I don't know what's keeping him alive.

Ray was sleeping away, but it wasn't long before he woke up and started making grimacing faces and was trying to flip around. He seems to be getting morphine more often now. I see little change in him, although I can't see how he can look worse than he does already. He's already skin and bones. He's still oozing from the holes in his stomach. He's all crippled up, like he has been for years. How much worse can someone be and still be alive?

I pleaded with God today, "Please don't make Ray suffer anymore. Why does he have to live anymore? Please, please take him." He hasn't answered my prayers so far. I don't see why He would answer them today, either.

March 16, Thursday

The vigil continues. Ray has been sleeping off and on for two hours. He must have exhausted himself last night. He hasn't had morphine since this morning, according to my mother. Let's see now, I've talked to Mom, Lynn, and Mike all on the phone in Ray's room.

Mom informed me that Dad still has a cold. This is the third day. Lynn wanted to get straight what days we'll be coming down this weekend. I'll get two days off in a row from seeing Ray again. And Mike, poor Mike, I can't remember why he called.

We're all getting run-down, and there's no end in sight. Not that I want my brother to die quickly, but I don't want him to suffer anymore. He doesn't seem to be in pain today, but he has this sick look on his face as if he's nauseated. No more smiles. No more playing toss with his zebra.

While Ray slept I tried to envision what he would have been like if he didn't have all of his ailments. He'd be tall and handsome with sparkling eyes and a head of thick, graying hair. He'd make people laugh. He'd be a charmer, with the ladies always chasing after him. He'd also be a protective older brother who would have taken me by the hand and shown me how to be a compassionate and understanding person, not by telling me, but by example.

Then I realized that Raymond already has done those things. He already has made people laugh. He already has the ladies coming after him. He already has taken me by the hand. He already has opened my eyes to so much that I wouldn't have seen if he didn't come back into my life. I already have more compassion for the handicapped, the elderly, and the incapacitated because of what I've experienced since Raymond became ill.

I feel as if that's Raymond's purpose on earth—to make people smile, to charm them, to make them more understanding. He doesn't have to be a whole person to do that. He just has to hold people's hands and smile at them. That's our Raymond. Is that what I'm supposed to do—to tell everyone Raymond has a purpose?

If Raymond, as handicapped as he is, has a purpose, then everyone must have a purpose. If everyone has a purpose, that means that everyone is important. I wouldn't have felt that way unless I spent hour after hour by Ray's side. It was all part of God's master plan. That must be why I was so compelled to write down everything that has happened to Ray. God must have been working through me from the very beginning, and I didn't even know it.

I don't feel comfortable leaving Ray with nurses and aides whom I don't know, yet I'm so, so exhausted. Laura is going to be on the pediatric side of Ray's floor for 1½ weeks. She'll be here on Sunday, and she comes in to hook up Ray to his artificial nutrition.

Ray seemed comfortable. At least he wasn't thrashing about and moaning like he was yesterday. I left Northbrook early and went home to bed.

March 17, Friday

Happy St. Patrick's Day! I'm so out of it. I never know what day of the week it is anymore. I was all dressed in brown before I remembered what day it was, and I couldn't go through my drawers while Mike was sleeping to look for something green. I found the green plastic bracelet that we got when Mike's sister died and donated her organs. That will have to do.

I opened my mail today to find a jury duty summons. I postponed it until September. I can't see Ray lasting that long, but nothing would surprise me anymore.

March 18, Saturday

Lynn gave me an update. Last night Ray had a fever of 102. The nurse came in and gave him a Tylenol suppository. An hour passed, and Lynn felt him. He was still burning up.

"I don't know what would have happened if I wasn't there," she said.

"Weren't they checking on him?" I asked.

"No, I had to keep being a pest," she said. "You'd think that they'd be checking on him, as bad as he was. He was awake for the entire seven hours that I was there. They gave him morphine twice while I was there. I went out to my car and got my overnight bag in case he got worse. I was thinking that, maybe with his fever spiking, this was it. He finally went to sleep and felt cooler, so I left. Today he seems better. Well, I'm just going to keep my stuff in Ray's closet.

If anyone wants to steal my stuff, let them. It's just some old sweat pants and t-shirts."

"Lynn, what's keeping him alive?" I asked.

"I don't know. The nurse was appalled by his stomach. I was in the room while she was changing him, and she saw how much stuff oozed out of those two holes when he moved. It's all red and irritated again. She said that she was going to talk to the doctor about putting a barrier on his skin, like Vaseline," Lynn said.

"I looked at it on Thursday," I said, "and I thought that it didn't look bad. It was still red, but maybe only an area not bigger than four inches around. Come to think of it, maybe he was lying on that side and I couldn't see all of the irritation."

"Well, it looks bad again," she said.

"Why can't they close up those holes?" I asked. "Of course, if they did that, they'd have to take him back to West End."

"Why didn't they do that before they sent him here?" she asked.

"Because he had that fissure and they were afraid he'd get a blood infection," I said.

"Well, he has one anyway," she said.

"Lynn, I think that he's going to hold on until the guardianship hearing," I said.

"Why do you say that, Pat?" she asked.

"Maybe this is part of Ray's master plan to show how ridiculous and sad and cruel this whole thing is," I replied. "If people like Ray could speak up for themselves, this wouldn't be happening. Why can't handicapped people be treated the same as everyone else?

"Maybe the reason why this happened was to bring Ray back to us, to his family. Can you imagine if they put Ray in that hospital next to his group home? How would we see him if he's an hour away? We wouldn't be staying with him like we're doing now. I think that God brought Ray back to us."

Lynn's not analytical like me. I think people are better off if they're not trying to figure out why things happen. Maybe that's why she's not neurotic like I am.

Lynn had nothing to add to my theory. She went on to more practical matters, "I called Mom and told her to stay home." Dad was still sick, and Mom had been coming to see Ray by herself. I think this is affecting Dad more than he's letting on. It's just one big energy drain on us all.

Today I'm playing catch-up on my writing about this whole mess. I thought that I'd be crying, but, so far, I'm not. I guess that it's true what they say: What doesn't kill you will make you stronger. I'm going to be a rock. No, I'm going to be a mountain. My family is going to be a whole mountain range.

Lynn called me again tonight to give me an update. After she hung up from talking to me, the aide came in to take Ray's temperature. It was 101 degrees. The nurse came in and gave Ray a Tylenol suppository. Lynn waited an hour, and Ray seemed like he was getting warmer.

Lynn said, "I went to get the nurse to ask her to take Ray's temperature again, and she said, 'It hasn't been an hour yet.' I told her that it's been more than an hour. The nurse left and didn't come back. No one came in to take his temperature. So, I heard Betty [the aide that reminds me of Alice from the Brady Bunch]. She was in another room. I stood outside that room and waited for her to come out. Then I asked her to take Ray's temperature. It had gone up by one degree. So, the nurse gave Ray an injection of something. I guess it's to take down his temperature."

"Yeah, Laura called me at home once to tell me that she was giving it to him because his temperature hadn't gone down after he had Tylenol," I told Lynn.

"They had different people working on the floor today," she said. "It just doesn't seem like Ray is getting the attention that he was before."

"Yeah, it seems as if, starting this week, they have less people on the floor and they're not checking on Ray as often as they used to," I agreed.

"Well, they have more new patients now. Betty was saying, 'They have new people I don't know now. At least I know Ray.'" Lynn said. Betty was another one of Ray's girlfriends.

"Maybe we should say something to Nancy on Monday," I said. "You would think that, with someone as sick as Ray, they would be checking on him more often. There used to be people coming by the room all of the time looking in and asking how everything was. Now they don't do that anymore. Hours go by without someone coming in."

"If it's more than just me who notices it, then there's a problem," she said.

"Yeah," I agreed. "You'd think that if someone like Ray has a temperature, they'd be in there every hour, checking."

"Well, I think that they make the rounds and take the temperatures of all of the patients," she said.

"But when you know that someone has a fever, especially when Ray's went up so high yesterday, you'd think that they'd be more vigilant," I said.

Now we have a new worry. After Ray was getting such good care, we have to worry about him being neglected when we're not there.

March 19, Sunday

I called the nurses' station about 10:30 this morning. The nurse on duty said that Ray's temperature was about 102 degrees. They just gave him Tylenol.

"My sister said that he was restless yesterday," I said.

"He's kind of restless today, too," the nurse said.

"Well," I said, "my parents are coming up this afternoon. I just wondered if there was a change in his condition."

"We'll be calling Dr. Patel to see if there's anything we can do," the nurse said.

I wanted to say: Like what? What could they do? They're already giving him a pain patch, morphine, and Tylenol. We don't want him on antibiotics, so what more can they do for him?

Later I called the phone in Ray's room, and my dad answered. "How's Ray?" I asked him.

"Well, Mom just went down to the nurses' station to see what was happening. Can you hear Ray?" he asked. I could hear him in the background, crying out. "Wait, Mom just came back from the nurses' station. Here she is," Dad said.

Her voice sounded shaken. "Well, he still has a fever, but the nurses said he's gotten everything that he can get. They said that they gave him Tylenol twice," Mom said.

"Did they give him morphine?" I asked.

"I don't know," she replied.

"They can also give him an injection to bring down the fever. I wonder if they gave him that. I know that you don't want to be a pain, but maybe you should ask when he last got morphine so that, when the three hours are up, you can go get the nurse to give it to him," I told her. I'm trying so hard not to sound like I'm bossing her around

"Well, yeah," she said. "I'm so mad. I feel like calling Albany, but they're probably not in session."

"Maybe you should," I said. "The list of legislators to contact is in the drawer [the snack drawer in Ray's dresser]. I haven't had time to find the name and addresses of our representatives. Well, if Ray's still bad when you want to leave, call me and I'll come in," I said.

While I was talking to Mom on my cell phone, Lynn called on my land phone. She was talking to Mike when I hung up. I gave her the update on Ray.

Then I told her, "Mom said that when she went to the nurses' station they said they had given Ray everything that he could have. I can't believe that they gave him everything prescribed and he's still so bad."

"Why can't they just give Ray morphine every three hours?" she asked. "That nurse who was so upset about Ray's stomach said that, if you let too much time lapse between doses, it takes time for it to take effect. If they just gave it to him every three hours, it wouldn't wear off and he wouldn't suffer so much."

"Maybe we'll have to talk to Nancy or Dr. Patel about putting it in his chart to give it every three hours. Or maybe since it's so controlled they can't do that," I said.

Mom called back. "Since I talked to you they came in and gave Ray Tylenol and morphine, and the nurse left the room and said, 'I'll have to give him something better.' She came back in and gave Ray a shot. Now he seems to be settling down," she said.

"See, they didn't give him everything that they could have. So, now he can have the morphine at, what, 4:00?" I asked.

"Yeah," she said.

"So, now do we have to call them every three hours to see if he gets it?" I asked. "When Ray first got there, he was getting all kinds of attention. Now they're ignoring him. It seems like just this past week that's been happening, since they started getting new nurses on Ray's floor."

"Today he has nurses I've seen before," she said.

"Then why are they ignoring Ray?" I asked.

"Maybe they're sick of us," she replied.

"But why do we have to keep looking for them to ask them to take care of Ray?" I asked.

I know that she didn't have answers. Maybe tomorrow I'll have a talk with Nancy. She must be getting so sick of me, but why do we have to start chasing after nurses again like at West End? I'm getting so sick of all of this.

March 20, Monday

It was my turn to see Ray tonight. He was doing something I've never seen before. He would wake up from his sleep, breathe really heavily, and then shake. Then he'd close his eyes as if he was resting. He did that again and again.

I went out and got the nurse, another one whom I had never seen before. She came into the room and looked at Ray resting peacefully. "Well, if he was in any kind of distress, his skin would be pale or purple. His skin is a nice, healthy color," she said. With that, she left the room.

Finally, Ray went into a deep, deep sleep. He was breathing heavily, rhythmically, a deep, restful breathing. I guess he was okay. He didn't wake up shaking anymore, so I assumed that whatever was bothering him had passed. I kissed him on the top of the head and said my goodbyes. Every day I say my goodbyes as if it may be my last. Tonight I asked Ray if he would send me feathers when he got to heaven, like Mike's father and sister, who passed away recently, have sent him.

March 21, Tuesday

Something in the back of my mind said that I should go to see Ray before I went to work, but he slept so peacefully last night that I thought he was making a comeback. For some reason, I was weepy today thinking about Ray. I had been so good about not crying this week.

My brother from Georgia called me at about 12:45 PM, not his usual time. He usually called me at the end of the work day, around 3:00 PM.

"Just wanted to see how things were going," he said.

"Same old, same old," I said. "Ray was so bad this weekend. He had a fever of over 100 on Friday, Saturday, and Sunday; then yesterday no fever. I keep asking him, 'Ray-Ray, what's going on?'"

We talked about 20 minutes, and then I went to lunch. I was going to cut my lunch short, but I thought, darn it, I'm going to finish eating. When I got back to my desk, I had a voice mail message.

It was my dad. He said to get to Northbrook as soon as possible. Ray was going fast. I called Ray's room, and my dad answered.

"He's gone," Dad said. His voice was cracking.

This wasn't how it was supposed to be. I wanted to be there to comfort Ray, to hold his hand. He had suffered for so long, and then, suddenly, it was over. You wait and prepare yourself for this moment. I knew that it was coming, and yet, when it finally did, still it hit me hard. This is what I wanted, for Ray to be at peace, and still it hit me hard. At least he didn't die alone.

I went over to tell my supervisor. She gave me a big hug. And, of course, my friend, Ginny, was there comforting me, too. My "Crying Corner" buddies were also giving me words of reassurance: "Will you be all right to drive?" "Do you want me to drive you?" "If you need anything, just call." We've all been through so much this past year.

After I composed myself, I rushed out of work as fast as I could. I don't even know if I shut down my computer.

I called Mike on the way to Northbrook to tell him the news. He had cooked the roast that I had defrosted and was going to make something else to go with it. "I'll cancel my 6:00 appointment and bring dinner over to your mom's and dad's about 5:30," he said. What a blessing he was.

I called my brother back. I had just spoken to him not even an hour before and told him that Ray was the same. Now I had to tell him that he was dead.

I parked by the back entrance of Northbrook because I didn't know how long I'd be there. I was walking through the long, long halls in the basement to get to the elevators to Ray's ward, and the peppy little black woman who cleaned on Ray's floor was coming by. She came up to me. She must have heard about Ray. "Are you all right?" she asked. I nodded and started crying. She gave me a big hug. "It's gonna be all right," she reassured me. "I'll see you upstairs in a little while." The workers there talk to you just like you're family.

I came off of the elevators onto Ray's floor, and there was the look of concern on everyone's faces. They didn't say anything, probably because they didn't know if I knew yet. I went into Ray's room, and my sister Lynn was there.

"How did you get here so fast?" I asked her.

"Something told me that I should call here, and Dad told me that Ray had died," she replied. "I just left. I didn't say anything to my boss. She was in with a client."

My mom told me what had happened. "We got here at about 1:00," she said. "He started gasping for breath, then shaking. I went out to the nurses' station to get someone and asked, 'Can't you do something for Ray?' I came back in here, and a few minutes later he passed away. He had a smile on his face just before he died."

"He must have seen Janet waiting for him," I said. It made me feel better that he was with someone who loved him and that in his final moments he wasn't crying out in pain. My biggest fear was that he would be alone when he passed on, and that hadn't happened.

"He went so fast," Lynn said, still in disbelief. "Laura said that his blood pressure would go down; that we would know when the time was near."

I reminded Lynn, "That's Ray. He did things in his own way. Remember? He's 'The Mystery Man.' That's what Laura called him."

"She'll be coming in soon," my mom added.

Dad replied, "Yeah, Laura starts at 3:00 PM." It was 2:30 PM.

A cart with two urns of coffee, tea, cream, and sugar was wheeled into Ray's room for us. I went into Ray's closet and pulled out the box of donut holes that an aide had hidden there last night and put them on the chart. Then I went into the first drawer of Ray's dresser and pulled out a breakfast bar. "Didn't you have lunch?" my dad asked. "You must take a lot of lunches. It seems like you're always at lunch when I call." I needed comfort food.

Nancy came into the room after her meeting.

I wanted to convey my gratitude for all that the staff did. "Thank you for taking such good care of my brother," I said.

"He was no trouble at all," she said to me. He really wasn't. He wasn't a pain in the butt like the woman across the hall who yelled constantly. I hadn't heard her lately. She must have been sent to a different facility.

We packed up all of Ray's things to take home with us—his TV, his clothes, his video tapes and DVDs, and all of his stuffed animals. For someone who couldn't move much, he had accumulated a lot of stuff.

An aide with braids all over her head went and got a wire cart, like a shopping cart, to put everything in and pushed it down to the elevators for us. She would wait at the back door for us and help us put everything into my van. These people are so good to us, so willing to go the extra mile.

Laura came rushing toward Ray's room. She had just started her shift in the pediatric section of the floor. Someone must have told her that Ray died. I'm sure that word had spread around the whole facility like wildfire. I know that we were being talked about.

Laura peeked into the room, but didn't go in. "I knew that something was going to happen when I wasn't here," she said. She hugged me and Lynn, and we thanked her for taking such good care of Ray.

After we loaded Ray's stuff into my van, Mom and Dad went home. Lynn and I headed back to Ray's room to wait until the doctor got there to pronounce Ray dead; then they would ready the body to take it to the morgue. The aide said that we wouldn't want to stay there for that because they wrap the body up in plastic. I just didn't want Ray to be lying alone until then. I still have a hard time leaving the body of a loved one alone. I should be used to it by now.

When Lynn and I got off the elevator on Ray's floor, we saw Laura coming out of a room behind the nurses' station, wiping her eyes. She must have been crying. I'm sure that hers weren't the only wet eyes in that facility that day. Raymond had a way of tugging at people's hearts.

The aides had been in to clean up Ray. His face, that was so gaunt, looked even worse with no color, but it wasn't filled with pain. His hair was the neatest I had ever seen it. And his crooked teeth were sparkling white. Lynn and I were joking about how good his teeth looked.

While Lynn went to the bathroom, I held Ray's hand for the last time. It was still warm.

I've seen three dead people this past year. I've always thought that I was weak and would handle the death of a loved one badly; that I'd fall apart. I'd bawl all over them and wouldn't be able to let them go. But I haven't done any of that. They all looked so peaceful after life left their bodies. I have to keep reminding myself that they're at rest in a beautiful place, and I wouldn't want to deny anyone that. Letting go is so, so hard.

"I won't be able to hold your hand anymore, Ray-Ray. You remember to send me feathers like I asked. No one has sent me feathers yet," I told him. They say that when someone passes to the other side, sometimes they send feathers—little, fluffy white feathers. They're angel feathers.

Lynn came out of the bathroom in Ray's room. I looked at her and said, "Whose hand am I going to hold now?" I had just lost my dearest brother, my second child, my buddy. Ray-Ray had become all of those things to me. Now I'll have to go on without ever again being blessed with his beautiful smile or feeling the warmth of his hand in mine.

"Pat, you can hold Mike's hand," she replied. "Well, you can in a few weeks when tax season is over."

The hospital staff came to ready Raymond's body for the morgue.

"Goodbye, buddy," I said, as I placed a kiss on my two fingers and touched them to Ray's warm forehead. As I walked out of the room, that all-too-familiar pang that I felt at leaving a loved one alone came again. You'd think that after three deaths it would get easier, but it doesn't. It's never easy.

Once at my parents' house, I called Mary and my brother from Massachusetts to tell them of Ray's death so that they could make plans to come in from out of town. We hope that the funeral will be on Saturday. My parents had already talked to the church about having a breakfast after the burial. We just don't know how many people will come. My parents don't realize how many people our family has touched. They don't think that anyone will care to come to the funeral because they didn't know Ray. I started naming off all of the people whom I thought would come, and the list got longer and longer.

I called Matt, our attorney, to tell him that Ray had passed away. "I'm sorry to hear that," he said.

"Will you tally up your bill and send it to my parents?" I asked him.

"I'll contact the courts and take care of everything," he replied.

"Will you send a bill to my parents?" I asked again.

"Don't worry about it," he said. I think that he's going to waive the fee because he feels badly about what happened to us.

My dad had already started making up the obituary. I had already written a eulogy. We've had so much time to think about this. I just don't know if I can read my eulogy without crying. I'll have to practice it over and over aloud to some poor soul with patience.

We had a scrumptious meal of roast with potatoes and gravy that Mike had made. It tasted so good. I can't get enough comfort food. Beans and beets heated up in the microwave rounded out the meal.

My parents' phone kept ringing and ringing. Mike must have been busy making calls while Lynn and I were at Northbrook, and those people were calling to give their condolences. After dinner, we sorted out Ray's things from Northbrook. Some of the tapes we would give to Northbrook for their children's ward. The clothes we're giving back to the group home. The blanket that I had made Ray, his stuffed animals, and his ratty old necktie are going to be put in Ray's coffin.

We were all tired and went home to get some rest. I had assignments. I was to get Ray's Social Security number from his hospital records. I knew that there was a reason why I kept records of everything connected with Ray. They have all come in handy. I also had to go on MapQuest to get directions from Ray's group home to the funeral home and/or to the church for the workers of Ray's group home who may want to attend the funeral. They all loved Ray and had, except for the months since last November, spent more time with him than we had.

After I did my assignments, I polished up my eulogy; then I went downstairs to Mike's office to read the eulogy to him. I got through the whole thing without crying, but I cried afterwards. "I wanted to be with him when he died," I told Mike.

"You were with him when he needed you," he said.

"I know. I said my goodbyes so many times because I didn't know if I would be with him when he died."

My one brother from Georgia is coming in on Thursday. My other brother will arrive sometime after he takes his dogs to the veterinarian. I don't know when Mary will be able to come in. It'll be good to have someone else to lean on.

March 22, Wednesday

Today was endless. Lynn and I met my parents at the funeral home. The undertaker was a family friend who lived down the block from my parents. We picked out a casket, a vault, did the wording on the death notice, picked out the memorial cards, and discussed how the family will see Raymond for one last time. Oh, so many details.

It's so exhausting, but I should be used to planning funerals by now. The burial plot was already paid for, but still the expense is exorbitant. I can't believe that they can be allowed to charge so much, but what choice does one have? In the end, the bill for a casket, making Ray look nice, and directing people at the funeral service and to the cemetery was $5,700.00. I couldn't imagine what the cost would have been if we had a wake or a viewing.

There are so many details that go into planning a funeral. It's overwhelming making all those decisions. There's the death notice for the paper, which paper to put it in, and how to word it. Since we weren't going to have a wake, did we want to put something in the notice about where to send donations? We decided to have donations go to the nursing home that Raymond was at. I'm glad that we have a way of giving back to a place that was so good to Ray.

Then there were the finances. How much was in the life insurance that my parents purchased for Raymond years ago? The state will give our family $776.97 toward funeral expenses. The state gives $600 a month for each ward for expenses, but barely more than that to bury them. What if a ward of the state has no family to pay for the rest of the funeral expenses? What happens to those poor people?

After the funeral home, we went to my parents' house to eat and make more phone calls.

Joe Griffin returned my phone call that I had made while at the funeral home. He stuck with us throughout everything and was the only person who was totally honest with me; the only one. I had asked what would happen to the money in Ray's expense account.

Joe answered, "After all of the Medicaid bills come in, there should be close to $1,000 left in Ray's account. A letter will come from Bee Makowski. All that you have to do is to keep receipts and submit them, and she will reimburse you. The money cannot be used for contributions."

"Can it be used to pay for things like a funeral breakfast?" I asked.

"Absolutely," he replied. "I was just filling out the paperwork. I have to send it in, and they have to do an investigation to see if everything was done properly." I didn't want to go there. I couldn't fathom who they were investigating. "Your mom was telling me that you and your sister were going to write some letters," he said.

"Well, we want to start a letter-writing campaign to get that law passed to give families rights in making end-of-life decisions for their loved ones who can't," I replied.

"Well, if there is anything I can do, just let me know," he offered.

"As a matter of fact, in a few weeks I was thinking of coming down and maybe taking you to lunch, and we can talk about if there is something that I can do so that what happened to Ray will not happen to anyone else," I said.

I honestly don't remember his response, because then we were talking about directions to Ray's funeral. My brain was exhausted by all of those details. I just wanted a day where I didn't have to think or make a single decision. I knew that it was the fatigue kicking in.

I practiced reading my eulogy to Lynn, Mom, and Dad. Darn, when I read it to Mike yesterday I didn't cry at all. Today I made it to the first paragraph and had to stop. Then I started reading it all over again and got to the third paragraph. I'll just have to keep reading it and, hopefully, I'll be so nervous in church that I won't break down.

Soon we were on our way to Ray's group home to pick up his things. Lynn wanted to take her car. She thought that we could fit all of Ray's things in her trunk. Something told me to take the van just in case there was more than we had anticipated.

When we got to the group home, Amy, the director, took us to a back room to show us Ray's things. There were two big storage tubs, about six big boxes, shelves, boxes of about 50 DVDs, DVD holders; and that wasn't all. Amy informed us, "Ray has some collectibles that I didn't pack because I didn't want to break them. Let me get a box. Should we wrap them in paper towels?" She went to a display case and started taking out lighthouses.

I was trying to condense all of Ray's things, so I asked, "Why don't we take some of Ray's t-shirts and wrap the breakables in them?" The collectibles were gingerly packed.

"I think that Ray has some stuff in the basement," Amy said. More stuff? How much more could there be? More boxes came out, loaded onto a wheelchair. I have a big van, but I was running out of room. The third seat in the back was put down. Boxes were put on top of that, and then put on the floor in the back, and then the smaller things were stuffed into every nook and cranny that was available. The box of breakables was put in the middle seat between Mom and Lynn. We marveled at everything that Ray had accumulated. The group home didn't want Ray's wheelchair. That would be left at Northbrook. We also inherited Ray's TV.

"Each consumer has a monthly expense of $600," Amy told us. "When the account gets to a certain amount, no more gets put in, so we buy things or we take them places." I guess Amy felt that she had to explain all of the years of accumulation that we had just packed in the van.

We talked with the group home staff about Ray for a little while. "We won't forget Ray for a long, long time," Amy said. He touched so many people with his gentle ways and his radiant smile.

They took a photo of Ray off of the wall and gave it to my mother. My dad gave them a box of chocolates and thanked them for taking such good care of Ray. Hugs were exchanged and, with that, we were off to eat at Molly's Eatery. I had been looking forward to stuffing my face with their down-home cooking all day. I don't care if my clothes don't fit anymore because I've gained 15 pounds since last October.

On the short way to Molly's I was thinking. If there was $600 each month in Ray's account that they had to spend or lose, why couldn't they have hired someone to sit with Ray while we couldn't, or to clean him up in the hospital, or to cut his hair? Why couldn't that money have paid for the ambulance ride to West End that one time they had to send poor Don from Ray's group home to take Ray there? Where is the logic here? Where is the compassion? Where is the fairness? My brain can't accept the stupidity of it all. Then I thought, we're talking about a state that can't pass a law to stop helpless people from unnecessary suffering. How can we expect them to pass laws to use money judiciously?

We had a lovely lunch and just enjoyed each other's company, something we haven't done in what seemed like a lifetime. We were sort of in limbo between the anguish of Ray's death and the sadness of his funeral, sort of in a holding pattern before the next onslaught of emotions hit.

When we got home, we unloaded all of the boxes and tubs and other paraphernalia. I looked at some of the stuff and just asked why. Why would Ray have underwear when he wore diapers all of the time? Why would Ray have shoes when his feet were so curled up that shoes couldn't be put on them? Why would he have a bathrobe? Why would he have so many DVDs whose story lines he couldn't understand and that didn't have any music or dancing that he thoroughly loved? "What a waste," I said to Lynn.

After taking all of Ray's belongings upstairs to my parents' spare bedroom, I went home to write my memoirs. As I'm writing this, I'm just realizing that this is an accumulation of everything over Ray's lifetime. Besides, who am I to judge the people who have taken care of my brother all of these years? He wouldn't have judged them. I need to let this one go. I can't fight every single battle.

I had to play just one game of spider solitaire for the night. Before going to bed, I had to call my mother-in-law while I was under control. She tried talking to me yesterday, and all I could do was blubber into the phone.

March 23, Thursday

Lynn was going into work to catch up on her bookkeeping. Her boss was a CPA and tax accountant, so this was the busiest time of year for them. I was to meet my parents at their house, then go to the church with them to plan the funeral Mass.

I pulled up in front of my parents' house, and my dad came walking up to my van alone. My parents thought that most of the Mass would be pre-arranged for them. I had been through enough funerals to know otherwise.

We got to the church rectory and were led by Sr. Josephina into a sitting room beautifully decorated in blue with Victorian furnishings. Then she directed Dad and me to sit at a dining-room-sized table in front of a notebook with about a hundred plastic-coated pages of readings from the Bible. She instructed us, "First, you have to pick a reading from the First Testament." I looked at Dad for some assistance.

"You go ahead and pick," he pleaded with me. Poor man, his brain must be tired. So was mine.

Sr. Josephina tried to help us. She said, "There aren't any that, when you hear them in Mass, you say, I'd like to have that at my funeral?" Dad shook his head no, and motioned to me to pick. I have a terrible memory when it comes to the Bible. There were way too many readings to sit and read each one, so I read the first paragraph of several until I came across one that I liked.

Then there were a few other details to be ironed out.

"Now, do you have any favorite songs?" Sr. Josephina asked us.

This part was easy. I said, "Oh, yes." 'On Eagle's Wings,' 'Ave Maria,' and 'Let There Be Peace on Earth.'" That was it. Please, please, please don't make me think of any more songs. My brain was so tired.

Sr. Josephina persisted, "We need one more. How about — — — ?" and she named some more songs. I don't even remember which one I picked. I just named one. I'm sorry, Ray. I should have been more meticulous about planning your funeral Mass, but I'm so, so tired.

Fr. Quinby entered the room and sat across from me. If I wasn't so overcome with fatigue, I would have noticed how youthful he was for a priest.

He asked if there was anything special that I wanted him to say in the homily. I said, "How about something like, 'Ray isn't suffering anymore'?" It was all that I could come up with. I told him about how Ray loved music, especially musicals, and how I would play musical DVDs and sing to him, and how he would smile.

When we left the rectory, Fr. Quinby said to me, "Your family has been through so much."

I said, "I know, but God has been with us all of the way." And He has. I can feel Him. When you're going through an ordeal that is harder than anything you could ever imagine going through, just pray. He'll be with you. If you sit still and quiet yourself, you can feel His essence all around you.

We hadn't ordered any flowers for Ray, and I felt that we should have some for us to put on his coffin at the grave site. When my brother from Georgia got into town, he and I went to the grocery store that had a beautiful floral department. My mother loves roses, so we thought that it might make her feel better if we got some for Ray. From the florist I got a list of what the different colors of the roses meant. White was for innocence and purity. That would be perfect for my parents. Yellow meant happiness and remembrance. Perfect for everyone else. We brought them to my parents' house. My mother smiled when she saw them. That's just the effect that we wanted.

My brother from Massachusetts came into town, followed by my sister Mary and her husband. Then we were on our way to the funeral home so that my family could view Ray for the last time. We went into a private room and saw Ray laid out in his casket. He was in his casual clothes. No suit or dress shirt for Ray.

Ray was perfect. His arms and legs were straight. His jaw was aligned with his mouth closed over his crooked teeth. That wasn't *my* Ray. *My* Ray was all crooked and imperfect, yet beautiful just the same.

All around Ray were his stuffed toys—the zebra, the Santa, the yellow and the red bears, and the pink, fluffy dog. Covering him was the psychedelic-colored blanket that I had made for him. I slipped in a photograph of the entire family—my parents, all of my brothers and sisters, their spouses, and their children. I put in the ghost that I made for Ray while he was at West End and his ratty old necktie from the hospital. Then I tucked in the blanket around Ray for the last time.

"You're pretty good at that," the funeral director said when he saw me adding things to the casket. I should be. I've had plenty of experience these past six months. We all said our final goodbyes to Ray. I wanted to hold Ray's hand for one last time, but I knew it would be cold and lifeless. "Bye, Ray-Ray. You'll be so happy now. Say hi to Janet," I told Ray, and patted his shoulder. It made a crinkling noise like paper crunching. Okay, no more touching. I blew Ray a kiss and turned to leave. I didn't look back because I knew I'd get that familiar pang at leaving a loved one alone.

March 25, Saturday—The Funeral

The sun shown brightly today, as if Ray was beaming down upon us from heaven. Mike, Paul, and I got to my parents' church early. I gave the roses to the funeral director with instructions: "The white ones are for my parents, and the yellow ones are for everyone else."

Once my dad arrived, he pointed me in the direction of where I could find Sr. Josephina, and we finalized information for the Mass. Mary was going to do one reading from the Bible. One brother would do another reading. Mike was going to read the Prayers of the Faithful. Lynn and her children were going to take the gifts of the hosts and wine to the priest. Our other brother was a pallbearer. All of Ray's brothers and sisters were able to participate in what we Christians should feel is a celebration of the deceased person's life and a celebration of what they will experience in heaven.

Finally, it was time to go into the church. Fr. Quinby doesn't believe that the family should walk into the church behind the casket. For that, I was glad. I've walked behind too many caskets this year. I always lose my cool when I do that.

Today my family walked quietly down the aisle and took our seats in the front of the church. Later, the pallbearers would bring Ray's casket to the front of the church.

My father had helped with the design of the church when it was built over 26 years ago. I was one of the first people married there.

Raymond would have loved this church. The pews were arranged in a semi-circle around the altar. Behind the altar was a massive stained-glass window from floor to ceiling. It depicted rays of sun shining down from heaven in shades of blue and white. Christ sat in the middle, flanked by Michael the archangel and the angel Gabriel. They were in white and gold. When the sun shines on that window, as it did today, it's breathtaking. It was a beautiful setting for a funeral for Raymond.

I looked around the church as we were waiting. My friend, Donna, sat on the right all by herself, far away, as if she were intruding. I went over to hug her and thank her for coming.

On the far left was Joe Griffin. He had said that he would stick with us through this whole thing, and he was keeping his word. Next to him was an aide whom I recognized from Ray's group home. They had one of the residents from Ray's home with them. "Janet [the aide from the group home] asked if it was okay if they were here," Mom told me.

"Mom, why would they even question if it was okay? Ray would've loved having them here," I said.

My in-laws and Lynn's in-laws were in the pews behind us. We were so lucky to have so many people in our lives who have given us support through our torment.

My mind can't accept the fact that I'm going through yet another funeral. Maybe it's a defense mechanism. I hoped that I shoved enough tissues into my jacket pocket. I have too much time to think during the Mass, and the songs and readings that I picked were real tearjerkers for me.

I cried during the opening song. Then again during the "Ave Maria." Though I usually sing, there was no way that I could today without choking on my tears. It was best just to keep my mouth shut.

When it came time for Fr. Quinby to do the homily after the reading of the gospel, he pulled out his guitar. My parents said that sometimes he sings during Mass, but I didn't expect this.

He began. "When Ray's sister, Pat, was telling me a little about him, she said that Ray loved watching musicals. One of his favorite ones was *The Sound of Music*. That happens to be one of my favorites, also. The part I like most is when Maria Von Trapp is teaching the children to sing."

Fr. Quinby strummed his guitar and started singing, " 'Doe, a deer, a female deer, ray, a drop of golden sun.' That was Ray, a drop of golden sun."

Lynn and I looked at each other and smiled. What a beautiful tribute to Ray. I hoped that he was up in heaven hearing Fr. Quinby singing. I knew that he would be smiling, just as he did when we sang to him at Northbrook. After that, I knew that I was going to be all right. I just had to think of Ray as a drop of golden sun.

After the homily, Mike read the Prayers of the Faithful that he and I had lovingly crafted a few days ago:

For Raymond, that he may find the peace and happiness that he so richly deserves in heaven;

For caretakers everywhere, that they may be guided by the same patience and compassion that was given to Raymond;

For families with handicapped or ailing members that they may be given strength to help them through their difficult times;

For government workers, that their decisions be influenced by God's message of empathy and righteousness for all people;

For the family and friends that Raymond's life has touched that they find strength and comfort in each other;

For Raymond's family that they find consolation in the fact that they will be one day joined in heaven with Raymond, his sister Janet, and all their loved ones who have gone before them.

The Mass was over, and I was called to give a eulogy. As I was going up to the podium, I prayed that I could get through it without crying. I'm usually fine at a funeral unless the person giving the eulogy breaks down and cries. Then I break down, too.

I got up to the podium, and the copy of my speech wasn't there like I was told it would be. I reached into my pocket for the copy I had put in there just in case the copy that was supposed to be on the podium wasn't. Darn, I had given that to Sr. Josephina to put in the book along with the readings. I left the podium and went back to the pew I had been sitting in to get a copy out of my purse, and then remembered I had left my purse in my van. I would have to wing it. The thought of that terrified me. Well, what else could I do?

I went back to the podium. The nun who was more or less keeping things going along and announcing who was doing what readings looked up at me from the pew next to the podium. She opened the folder that she had been holding, the one that had been on the podium. She flipped it to the last page. There was my speech. "I'm sorry, I wasn't aware that it was there," she apologized.

What a relief. I put the folder back up on the podium and looked at the congregation. "Okay, everything is under control now," I said. I don't know where my newfound self-confidence came from, but I was as cool as a cucumber up there in front of everyone. I went on with the eulogy:

> Raymond was born on May 28, 1951. I wasn't around yet, but I've been told that he was a beautiful baby boy. Over the years, Raymond's multiple ailments took a toll on his body, but never on his spirit. He survived beyond everyone's expectations and fought until the bitter end with a strength unsurpassed by most healthy people. I have no idea where that stubbornness came from.

> Many would ask why God puts people like Raymond on this earth. What would be the purpose of a life where one couldn't communicate, couldn't walk, and, in the end, couldn't even do his favorite

thing—eat? We may have to reach heaven before we get an answer to that question, but my theory is that Raymond was put on this earth to make us better people. And what better example of unconditional love could we experience than Raymond? He loved everyone and judged no one. He had a smile for anyone who would pay the slightest bit of attention to him. He would grin from ear to ear if he was put in the midst of people, like he was going on a great adventure.

"I'd like to interject a little story about Ray," I continued. Never in a million years would I have done that before today. My ordeal with Ray had given me strength I could never have imagined. I think Raymond's spirit was already working through me. There I was up near the altar in front of all those people, ad-libbing a story about Ray. Maybe it was because I was talking about Ray, and that made my insides smile and chased away any nervousness I had, but I could do no wrong when I was up there talking about him.

I told the crowd about when Ray was being taken on the gurney to West End to have his PICC line re-inserted and how the ambulance attendant told Ray to cheer up. That picture of him smiling as he was being wheeled away will be with me forever. I heard a few chuckles from the crowd. That was Ray, always making people smile. I went on with the eulogy.

Raymond was a people person, and he brought out the good in all of us. There was no one that met Ray who wasn't affected by his gentle nature and that big, beautiful smile. He never knew how many people cared about him and prayed for him. He never knew the outpouring of love that came from so many people because of him. Because everybody loved Raymond.

(This is where I usually cried when I practiced reading in front of my family, but I didn't today. I knew that Ray was at peace and that made me feel good. I just went on.)

> We can all take comfort in the fact that Raymond is now up in heaven, a whole person who can run, and talk, and eat as much as he wants. I hope that God is ready for this, because Raymond is now up in heaven wreaking havoc with his sister Janet, and heaven will never be the same.

The funeral had concluded. It was a Mass that Ray certainly deserved. I couldn't remember a more beautiful funeral Mass. Everything was perfect and uplifting and just so special. Raymond was given in death what we couldn't give him at the end of his life.

It was a long ride to the cemetery. My parents' plots were in a section under a grove of majestic maple trees. Ray was to be buried next to my sister, Janet, who was killed by a drunk driver, over 25 years ago. My Aunt Trudie was buried second from the last of the six plots that my parents had purchased way back when Ray was a little boy. I'm sure that they couldn't foresee back then that three people would be buried in those plots before they would be. Thank God that we have no premonition of what life will bring.

After a short reading and a blessing for Ray, we each took a rose and put it on Ray's casket. I placed a final kiss on my fingers and touched it to Ray's coffin. As we walked across the cemetery grounds, we were graced with a breeze that had the fresh smell of hope for better weather, just as we had the fresh hope for a better life for Raymond in heaven.

I looked around and saw that even though it was March, spring was upon us. The winter had whizzed by so quickly. The grass was starting to turn green. The spring flowers were poking their shoots out of the ground. It was as if God had orchestrated the early beginning of a new growth season to remind us that now was the time for a new beginning for our lives also.

I'm confident that my life will take a new direction because of what I've experienced over the past few months. I want to help those who have no one else fighting for them. Perhaps I will do that by becoming involved in politics and helping to get the Family Health Care Decisions Act passed to help incapacitated people and their families. Perhaps I will become an advocate or a lobbyist for the handicapped. Or, perhaps I will just hold the hand of someone who has no one else to hold their hand.

As I got in my van to go back to the funeral breakfast at my parent's church, I thanked God for bringing Raymond back into my life. I saw those days as a gift. Raymond is gone but his spirit will live on in the lessons I've learned from him in his final days.

I realized how important his life was, and through that I saw how important *every* life is. I learned that he had a purpose for being here, and through that I saw that *every* person must have a purpose. Now I look upon *everyone* as a gift to the world. And a gift is something that should be cherished.

Raymond showed me all of that without uttering a single word or writing a single phrase. He did it with his gentle nature and his big, beautiful smile. That smile has launched me on a journey that has just begun.

Epilogue

$\mathcal{A}$ web site has been set up by the author's family to tell Raymond's story, to educate others on the New York State laws regarding withdrawal of life sustaining treatment, and to encourage people to urge their New York State legislators to pass ethical laws regulating withdrawal of life sustaining treatment.

For important up-to-date information and links to pertinent web sites, please visit www.arayofhope.info.

On March 14, 2010, after nearly two decades of first being introduced in the state legislature the Family Health Care Decisions Act was signed into law. That law gives every New York State resident the right to make end-of-life decisions when their loved ones became incapicitated

I feel that Raymond and his story had a hand in passing this important piece of legislation so others wouldn't suffer as he did

Printed in the United States
203625BV00003B/277-387/A

9 781602 667648